P9-DDC-415

Pocket
CHICAGO
TOP SIGHTS • LOCAL LIFE • MADE EASY

Karla Zimmerman

In This Book

QuickStart Guide

Your keys to understanding the city – we help you decide what to do and how to do it

Need to Know
Tips for a smooth trip

Neighborhoods
What's where

Explore Chicago

The best things to see and do, neighborhood by neighborhood

Top Sights
Make the most of your visit

Local Life
The insider's city

The Best of Chicago

The city's highlights in handy lists to help you plan

Best Walks
See the city on foot

Chicago's Best...
The best experiences

Survival Guide

Tips and tricks for a seamless, hassle-free city experience

Getting Around
Travel like a local

Essential Information
Including where to stay

Our selection of the city's best places to eat, drink and experience:

◉ Sights

✖ Eating

🅟 Drinking

✪ Entertainment

🅐 Shopping

These symbols give you the vital information for each listing:

☏ Telephone Numbers	👪 Family-Friendly
⊙ Opening Hours	🐾 Pet-Friendly
🅟 Parking	🚌 Bus
⊖ Nonsmoking	⛴ Ferry
@ Internet Access	Ⓜ Metro
📶 Wi-Fi Access	Ⓢ Subway
🥬 Vegetarian Selection	🚋 Tram
📖 English-Language Menu	🚆 Train

Find each listing quickly on maps for each neighborhood:

Bar Hemingway

16 🅟 Map p233, B2

Legend has it that Hemi self, wielding a machine rate this timber-pan tered bar during showpiece is a en by Papa ar town. Dress s.com; Hôtel Rit ; ⊙6.30pm-2a

Lonely Planet's Chicago

Lonely Planet Pocket Guides are designed to get you straight to the heart of the city.

Inside you'll find all the must-see sights, plus tips to make your visit to each one really memorable. We've split the city into easy-to-navigate neighborhoods and provided clear maps so you'll find your way around with ease. Our expert authors have searched out the best of the city: walks, food, nightlife and shopping, to name a few. Because you want to explore, our 'Local Life' pages will take you to some of the most exciting areas to experience the real Chicago.

And of course you'll find all the practical tips you need for a smooth trip: itineraries for short visits, how to get around, and how much to tip the guy who serves you a drink at the end of a long day's exploration.

It's your guarantee of a really great experience.

Our Promise

You can trust our travel information because Lonely Planet authors visit the places we write about, each and every edition. We never accept freebies for positive coverage, so you can rely on us to tell it like it is.

QuickStart Guide 7

Explore Chicago 21

Worth a Trip:

QuickStart Guide

Welcome to Chicago

Take cloud-scraping architecture, lakefront beaches and world-class museums, stir in wild comedy, fret-bending guitars and very hefty pizza, and you've got a town that won't let you down. The city center is a steely wonder, but it's Chicago's mural-splashed neighborhoods – with their inventive storefront restaurants, fringe theaters and sociable dive bars – that really blow you away.

Chicago skyline from below
JOE DANIEL PRICE/GETTY IMAGES ©

Chicago
Top Sights

Art Institute of Chicago (p28)

Marble halls filled with masterpieces.

Millennium Park
(p24)

Park with whimsical public art.

Willis Tower (p30)

Views from Chicago's loftiest skyscraper.

Wrigley Field (p80)

Iconic ballpark full of tradition.

Field Museum of Natural History (p114)

Mammoth and extensive museum.

360° Chicago (p56)

Views high in the sky.

Lincoln Park (p68)

Chicago's biggest park and playground.

Navy Pier (p44)

Carnival on the wharf.

Museum of Contemporary Art (p58)

Museum of audacious, thought-provoking works.

Chicago Local Life

Local experiences and hidden gems to help you uncover the real city

After checking off Chicago's top sights, seek out the bohemian jazz clubs, brainy bookstores, doughnut bakeries and arty shops that make up the locals' Windy City. Count on neon-bathed dive bars and cool galleries also popping up.

KRIS DAVIDSON/LONELY PLANET ©

Mixing It Up in Andersonville & Uptown (p86)
☑ Antique shops ☑ Al Capone's speakeasy

A Night Out in Logan Square (p99)
☑ Neighborhood bars ☑ Street art

West Loop Wander (p102)

☑ Hip cafes ☑ Contemporary art

Other great places to experience the city like a local:

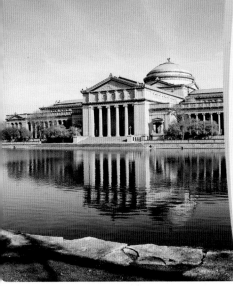

A Bookish Day in Hyde Park (p124)

☑ Scholarly bookstores ☑ Famous architecture

Chicago
Day Planner

Day One

You might as well dive right in with the big stuff in the Loop. Take a boat or walking tour with the **Chicago Architecture Foundation** (p146) and ogle the most sky-scraping collection of buildings the US has to offer. Saunter over to **Millennium Park** (p24) to see 'the Bean' reflect the skyline and to splash under Crown Fountain's human gargoyles.

Stay in the Loop for lunch. The **Gage** (p36) dishes out pub grub with an inventive twist. Explore the **Art Institute of Chicago** (p28), the nation's second-largest art museum. It holds masterpieces aplenty. Next head over to **Willis Tower** (p30), zip up to the 103rd floor and step out onto the glass-floored ledge. Yes, it is a long way down.

The West Loop parties in the evening. Walk along Randolph St and take your pick of hot-chef restaurants, such as **Roister** (p106) or **Little Goat** (p106). Bars are chockablock too. **Haymarket Pub & Brewery** (p103) pours great beers. Or sit on the glittery patio sipping a glass of bubbly at **RM Champagne Salon** (p109).

Day Two

Begin in the Near North with a stroll on Michigan Ave – aka the **Magnificent Mile** (p48) – where big-name department stores ka-ching in a glittering row. Mosey over to **Navy Pier** (p44). Take a spin on the high-in-the-sky Ferris wheel and heft a mighty slice of pizza at **Giordano's** (p45).

Spend the afternoon at the South Loop's Museum Campus (the water taxi from Navy Pier is a fine way to get there). Miles of aisles of dinosaurs and gemstones stuff the **Field Museum** (p114). Sharks and other fish swim in the kiddie-mobbed **Shedd Aquarium** (p118). Meteorites and supernovas are on view at the **Adler Planetarium** (p118).

Hop the Blue Line to Damen for a meal at retro diner **Dove's Luncheonette** (p92) in Wicker Park. Wander along Milwaukee Ave and take your pick of booming bars, indie-rock clubs and hipster shops. **Quimby's** (p96) shows the local spirit: the bookstore stocks zines and graphic novels, and is a linchpin of Chicago's underground culture. The **Hideout** (p95) and **Empty Bottle** (p95) are sweet spots to catch a bad-ass band.

Short on time?
We've arranged Chicago's must-sees into these day-by-day itineraries to make sure you see the very best of the city in the time you have available.

Day Three

☀ Get some fresh air this morning. Dip your toes in Lake Michigan at **North Avenue Beach** (p72). Amble northward through the sprawling greenery of **Lincoln Park** (p68). Stop at **Lincoln Park Zoo** (p72) to see lions, zebras and bears (the polar kind). Pop into **Lincoln Park Conservatory** (p73) to smell exotic blooms.

☀ Make your way north to **Wrigley Field** (p80) for an afternoon baseball game. The atmospheric, century-old ballpark hosts the Cubs, a team that had been cursed for a century but whose fortune, recently, changed. Afterward have a beer at **Gman Tavern** (p83) or one of the many rowdy bars that circle the stadium.

☽ Head to Andersonville & Uptown in the evening. Hmm, mussels and *frites* at **Hopleaf** (p87), or southern-style chicken and dumplings at **Big Jones** (p87)? Andersonville has several fine taverns to hang out at and sink a pint, like **Simon's** (p87). Jazz hounds can venture to the **Green Mill** (p87), a timeless venue to hear jazz, watch a poetry slam or swill a martini. Al Capone used to groove at it.

Day Four

☀ You can learn a lot in Hyde Park. The **Museum of Science & Industry** (p125) isn't kidding around with its acres of exhibits. There's a German U-boat, mock tornado and exquisite dollhouse for starters. Groovy university bookstores like **Seminary Co-op** (p125) and **Powell's** (p125) offer shelves of weighty tomes. Architecture buffs can tour **Robie House** (p125), Frank Lloyd Wright's Prairie-style masterpiece. Have lunch at Valois Cafe, Obama's old hangout.

☀ See what's going on in the chichi Gold Coast. There's boutique shopping, of course. The **Museum of Contemporary Art** (p58) always has something odd and provocative showing. And you can't leave the 'hood without getting high. For that, ascend to the 94th-floor observatory at **360° Chicago** (p56) or the 96th-floor **Signature Lounge** (p64).

☽ Spend the evening among locals in hip-happening Logan Square. Sip whiskey while waiting for a table at **Longman & Eagle** (p99). Knock back slurpable beers at **Revolution Brewing** (p99). See what arty band is playing for free at wee **Whistler** (p99).

Need to Know

**For more information,
see Survival Guide (p147)**

Currency
US dollar ($)

Language
English

Visas
Generally not required for stays of up to 90 days for visitors from most EU countries, Japan, Australia and New Zealand. Check www.state.gov/travel for details.

Money
ATMs widely available. Credit cards accepted at most hotels, restaurants and shops.

Cell Phones
The only foreign phones that will work in the US are multiband GSM models. Buy prepaid SIM cards or a cheap pay-as-you-go phone locally.

Time
Central Standard Time (GMT/UTC minus six hours)

Tipping
Expected at most places. Restaurant servers: 15% to 20%. Bartenders: 15% per round (minimum per drink $1). Porters: $2 per bag. Housekeeping staff: $2 to $5 per night. Taxi drivers 10% to 15%.

❶ Before You Go

Your Daily Budget

Budget: Less than $100
► Dorm bed: $35–50
► Lunch specials: $10–15
► Transit day pass: $10

Midrange: $100–300
► Hotel or B&B double room: $150–250
► Dinner in a casual restaurant: $25–35
► Architecture boat tour: $46

Top end: More than $300
► Luxury hotel double room: $400
► Dinner at Alinea: $285
► Lyric Opera ticket: $200

Useful Websites

Lonely Planet (www.lonelyplanet.com/chicago) Destination information, hotel bookings, traveler forum and more.

Choose Chicago (www.choosechicago.com) Official tourism site with sightseeing and event info.

DNA Info Chicago (www.dnainfo.com/chicago) Detailed news about sights, bars, restaurants and events, broken down by neighborhood.

Advance Planning

Two months before Book your hotel. Reserve at mega-hot restaurants such as Alinea and Girl & the Goat.

Two weeks before Reserve a table at your other must-eat restaurants, and book tickets for sports events and blockbuster museum exhibits.

One week before Check www.hottix.org for half-price theater tickets.

② Arriving in Chicago

O'Hare International Airport (ORD; www.flychicago.com) is 17 miles northwest of downtown. Chicago Midway Airport (MDW; www.flychicago.com) is 11 miles southwest of downtown. O'Hare is bigger and handles most of the international flights. Both airports have easy El train links into the city.

From O'Hare International Airport

The Blue Line El train ($5) runs 24/7 and departs every 10 minutes or so. The journey to the city center takes 40 minutes. Shuttle vans cost $35, taxis around $50.

From Chicago Midway Airport

The Orange Line El train ($3) runs between 4am and 1am, departing every 10 minutes or so. The journey takes 30 minutes to downtown. Shuttle vans cost $30, taxis $35 to $40.

From Union Station

All trains arrive at this huge station at the Loop's western edge. For transportation onward, the Blue Line Clinton stop is a few blocks south (thought it's not a great option at night). Taxis queue along Canal St outside the station entrance.

③ Getting Around

The El (a system of elevated and subway trains) is the main way to get around. Buses are also useful. Buy a day pass for $10 at El stations. The Chicago Transit Authority (www.transitchicago.com) runs the transport system.

🚆 Train

The El (it stands for 'elevated,' though many trains also run underground) is fast and frequent. Red and Blue Lines operate 24/7. The other lines run from 4am to 1am daily. The standard fare is $3 (except from O'Hare airport, where it costs $5).

🚌 Bus

Buses cover areas that the El misses. Most run at least from early morning until 10pm; some go later. Some don't run on weekends. The fare is $2 ($2.25 if you want a transfer).

🚕 Taxi

Taxis are easy to find downtown, north to Andersonville and west to Wicker Park/Bucktown. It costs $3.25 when you get into the cab, then $2.25 per mile. Uber, Lyft and Via are also popular in the city.

🚲 Bicycle

Lots of locals cycle to get around. Divvy bike-share stations are ubiquitous; a 24-hour pass costs $10. Bike rentals for longer rides (with accoutrements such as helmets and locks) start at around $18 for two hours.

Chicago
Neighborhoods

Wrigley
Field
⊙

Lake View & Wrigleyville (p78)
Baseball lovers and nightlife fans share the bar-filled neighborhood, which parties hard, especially in club-thumping Boystown.

⊙ **Top Sights**

Wrigley Field

Lincoln Park & Old Town (p66)
Beaches and zoo animals, top eateries and stylish shops abound in Lincoln Park, while Old Town has Second City comedy.

⊙ **Top Sights**

Lincoln Park

Wicker Park, Bucktown & Ukrainian Village (p88)
Few sights, but you can easily spend the day here shopping and the night eating, drinking and hitting the myriad rock clubs.

Near West Side & Pilsen (p100)
Buzzy, top-chef restaurants are the Near West Side's calling card. Mexican taquerias meet hipster hangouts in Pilsen.

Worth a Trip

○ **Local Life**

Mixing It Up in Andersonville & Uptown (p86)

A Night Out in Logan Square (p98)

A Bookish Day in Hyde Park (p124)

Gold Coast (p54)
Furs and Rolls Royces are de rigueur, as are swanky boutiques and cocktail lounges.

◉ **Top Sights**
360° Chicago

Museum of Contemporary Art

Near North & Navy Pier (p42)
Shops, restaurants, hotels, galleries, boats and amusements abound in this densely packed quarter.

◉ **Top Sights**
Navy Pier

The Loop (p22)
Chicago's center of action for both business and play, with skyscrapers galore.

◉ **Top Sights**
Millennium Park

Art Institute of Chicago

Willis Tower

South Loop & Near South Side (p112)
The South Loop bustles with the lakefront Museum Campus. Blues sights and Chinatown are further on.

◉ **Top Sights**
Field Museum of Natural History

Lincoln Park ◉

360° Chicago ◉

Museum of Contemporary Art ◉

Navy Pier ◉

Millennium Park ◉

Willis Tower ◉

Art Institute of Chicago ◉

Field Museum of Natural History ◉

Explore
Chicago

Worth a Trip

Millennium Park (p24)
CHUCK ECKERT/GETTY IMAGES ©

Explore

The Loop

The Loop is Chicago's center of action – its financial and historic heart – and it pulses with energy. Tumultuous tides of pinstriped businessfolk rush the sidewalks, while clattering El trains roar overhead. But it's not all work here. The Loop is also Chicago's favorite playground. The Art Institute, Willis Tower, Theater District and Millennium Park are top draws among the skyscrapers.

The Sights in a Day

☼ There's lots to see in the Loop. Get an early start at the **Art Institute** (p28), then wander around and explore the neighborhood's art and architecture. The **Chicago Cultural Center** (p34) and **Daley Plaza** (p34) are eye poppers.

☀ Grab a quick lunch at **Revival Food Hall** (p37) or **Shake Shack** (p38). Active types can rent two-wheelers at **Bike Chicago** (p34) or kayaks from **Urban Kayaks** (p36) and set off on DIY explorations. Late afternoon is usually less crowded for an ascent up **Willis Tower** (p30) to its unnerving glass ledges. Phew. You'll need a drink after that, so it's handy the **Berghoff** (p38) is down the road.

☾ Stop at **Pastoral** (p37) for picnic fixings, then take the spread to **Millennium Park** (p24) for the free evening concert. **Grant Park Orchestra** (p39) zings the strings there three times a week. **Lyric Opera** (p41) and **Goodman Theatre** (p39) are other entertainment options. For dinner, try **Gage** (p36) for smart gastropub fare or **Pizano's** (p37) for deep-dish pizza.

👁 Top Sights

Millennium Park (p24)

Art Institute of Chicago (p28)

Willis Tower (p30)

🖤 Best of Chicago

Architecture

Willis Tower (p30)

Rookery (p35)

Chicago Cultural Center (p34)

Eating

Revival Food Hall (p37)

Pizano's (p37)

Native Foods Cafe (p37)

Museums & Galleries

Art Institute of Chicago (p28)

Money Museum (p35)

Drinking

Cindy's (p39)

Sports & Activities

Bike Chicago (p34)

Urban Kayaks (p36)

Getting There

Ⓜ **El** All lines converge in the Loop. Clark/Lake is a useful transfer station between them. Washington/Wabash is handy for the parks, Quincy for Willis Tower.

Top Sights
Millennium Park

Chicago's showpiece shines with whimsical public art. Where to start amid the mod designs? Perhaps Pritzker Pavilion, Frank Gehry's swooping silver band shell. Jaume Plensa's Crown Fountain, with its human gargoyles. Anish Kapoor's silvery sculpture *Cloud Gate* (aka 'the Bean'). Or maybe someplace away from the crowds, like the veiled Lurie Garden abloom with prairie flowers.

👁 Map p32, F2

☎ 312-742-1168

www.millenniumpark.org

201 E Randolph St

🕙 6am-11pm

Ⓜ Brown, Orange, Green, Purple, Pink Line to Washington/Wabash

Lurie Garden (p26), Millennium Park

Magic Bean

The park's biggest draw is 'the Bean' – officially titled *Cloud Gate* – Anish Kapoor's 110-ton, silver-drop sculpture. It reflects both the sky and the skyline, and everyone clamors around to take a picture and to touch its silvery smoothness. Good vantage points for photos are at the sculpture's northern and southern ends. For great people-watching, go up the stairs on Washington St, on the Park Grill's northern side, where there are shady benches.

Crown Fountain

Jaume Plensa's Crown Fountain is another crowd-pleaser. Its two, 50ft-high, glass-block towers contain video displays that flash a thousand different faces. The people shown are all native Chicagoans and they all agreed to strap into Plensa's special dental chair, where he immobilized their heads for filming. Each mug puckers up and spurts water, just like the gargoyles atop Notre Dame Cathedral. A fresh set of nonpuckering faces appears in winter, when the fountain is dry. On hot days the fountain crowds with locals splashing in the streams to cool off. Kids especially love it.

Pritzker Pavilion at Night

Pritzker Pavilion is Millennium Park's acoustically awesome band shell. Architect Frank Gehry designed it and gave it his trademark swooping silver exterior. The pavilion hosts free concerts at 6:30pm most nights June to August. There's indie rock, world music and jazz on Monday and Thursday, and classical music on Wednesday, Friday and Saturday. On Tuesday there's usually a movie beamed onto the huge screen on stage. Seats are available up close in the pavilion, or you can sit on the grassy Great Lawn that unfurls behind.

☑ Top Tips

▶ The Family Fun Tent in the park's northwest corner offers free arts, crafts and games for kids between 10am and 2pm daily in summer.

▶ Concessions, bathrooms and a gift shop are available at McCormick Tribune Plaza (by the outdoor cafe/ice rink) on Michigan Ave.

▶ Volunteers provide free walking tours of the park at 11:30am and 1pm daily from late May to mid-October. Departure is from the Chicago Cultural Center's Randolph St lobby, across the road at 77 E Randolph St. Space is limited to 10 people on a first-come, first-served basis.

....

✗ Take a Break

A burger and creamy caramel milkshake at Shake Shack (p38) will provide fuel for more sightseeing. Go French with a baguette and cafe au lait at Toni Patisserie & Cafe (p38).

Picnic Time

For all shows – but especially the classical ones, which the top-notch Grant Park Orchestra performs – folks bring blankets, picnics, wine and beer. There is nothing quite like sitting on the lawn, looking up through Gehry's wild grid and seeing all the skyscraping architecture that forms the backdrop while hearing the music. If you want a seat up close, arrive early.

Pritzker Pavilion by Day

The pavilion also hosts daytime action. Concert rehearsals take place Tuesday to Friday, usually from 11am to 1pm, offering a taste of music if you can't catch the evening show. Each Saturday free exercise classes turn the Great Lawn into a groovy fitness center. Instructors backed by live music-makers lead Pilates at 7am, yoga at 8am, strength training at 9am and Zumba dance at 10am.

Lurie Garden

If the crowds at the Bean, Crown Fountain and Pritzker Pavilion are too much, seek out the peaceful **Lurie Garden** (www.luriegarden.org), which uses native plants to form a botanical tribute to Illinois' tallgrass prairie. Visitors often miss the area, because it's hidden behind a big hedge. Yellow coneflowers, poet's daffodils, bluebells and other gorgeous blooms carpet the 5-acre oasis; everything is raised sustainably and without chemicals. A little river runs through it, where folks kick off their shoes and dangle their feet.

From mid-May to mid-September, volunteers lead free tours through the garden on Thursday and Friday between 11am and 1:15pm, and on Sunday between 11am and 2:15pm. They last 20 minutes and depart every 15 to 20 minutes. No reservations are required, just show up at the southern end of the boardwalk.

BP Bridge & Nichols Bridgeway

In addition to Pritzker Pavilion, Frank Gehry also designed the snaking BP Bridge that spans Columbus Dr. The luminous sheet-metal walkway connects Millennium Park (from the back of the Great Lawn) to the new Maggie Daley Park (p34), which has ice-skating and rock climbing among its activity arsenal. The bridge offers great skyline views too.

The Nichols Bridgeway is another pedestrian-only span. Renzo Piano designed this silver beauty. It arches from the park over Monroe St to the Art Institute's 3rd-floor contemporary sculpture terrace (which is free to view). Piano, incidentally, also designed the museum's Modern Wing, which is where the sculpture terrace is located.

Cycling & Ice Skating

The McDonald's Cycle Center, in the park's northeastern corner near the intersection of Randolph St and Columbus Dr, is the city's main facility for bike commuters, with 300

McCormick Tribune Ice Rink

bike-storage spaces plus showers. It's also a convenient place to pick up rental bikes from Bike Chicago (p34), including road, hybrid, tandem and children's bikes.

Tucked between the Bean sculpture and the twinkling lights of Michigan Ave, the **McCormick Tribune Ice Rink** fills with skaters in winter. It operates from late November to late February and it is hands down the city's most scenic rink. Admission is free; skate rental costs $12. In summer the rink morphs into the Park Grill's alfresco cafe.

Wrigley Square & Boeing Galleries

The big plaza at the corner of Michigan Ave and Randolph St is Wrigley Square. The Greek-looking structure rising up from it is the Millennium Monument. It is a replica of the original peristyle that stood here between 1917 and 1953. The semi circular row of Doric columns shoots up nearly 40ft. It juxtaposes oddly with the modern art throughout the rest of the park, but it's meant to tie past and present together. The lawn in front is dandy for lolling.

Top Sights
Art Institute of Chicago

The second-largest art museum in the country, the Art Institute houses a treasure trove from around the globe. The collection of impressionist and postimpressionist paintings is second only to those in France, and the number of surrealist works is tremendous. The Modern Wing dazzles with Picassos and Mirós, while Japanese prints, Grecian urns and suits of armor stuff endless rooms beyond.

◉ Map p32, F4

www.artic.edu

111 S Michigan Ave

adult/child $25/free

🕙10:30am-5pm Fri-Wed, to 8pm Thu

Ⓜ Brown, Orange, Green, Purple, Pink Line to Adams

Must-See Works: Floor 2

Get close enough to Georges Seurat's *A Sunday Afternoon on the Island of La Grande Jatte* (Gallery 240) for the painting to break down into its component dots and you'll see why it took Seurat two long years to complete his pointillist masterpiece. *Nighthawks* (Gallery 262), Edward Hopper's lonely, poignant snapshot of four solitary souls at a neon-lit diner, was inspired by a Greenwich Ave restaurant in Manhattan. Grant Wood, a lifelong resident of Iowa, used his sister and his dentist as models for the two stern-faced farmers in his iconic painting *American Gothic* (Gallery 263).

Must-See Works: Floors 1 & 3

America Windows (Gallery 144) – huge, blue stained-glass pieces – were created by Marc Chagall to celebrate the USA's bicentennial. The elongated figure of *The Old Guitarist* (Gallery 391) by Pablo Picasso is from the artist's Blue Period, reflecting not only Picasso's color scheme but also his experience as a poor, lonely artist in Paris in the early years. Salvador Dalí's *Inventions of the Monsters* (Gallery 396) was painted in Austria immediately before the Nazi annexation. The title refers to a Nostradamus prediction that the apparition of monsters presages the outbreak of war.

Other Intriguing Sights

The Thorne Miniature Rooms (Lower Level, Gallery 11) and Paperweight Collection (Lower Level, Gallery 15) are awesome, overlooked galleries. In the light-drenched Modern Wing, the ongoing exhibition 'The New Contemporary' (Galleries 288 and 290–99) bursts with iconic works by Andy Warhol, Roy Lichtenstein and Jasper Johns.

☑ **Top Tips**

▶ Allow two hours to browse the museum's highlights; art buffs should allocate much longer.

▶ Advance tickets are available (surcharge $2), but unless there's a blockbuster exhibit going on they're usually not necessary. The entrance queue moves fast.

▶ Ask at the information desk about free talks and tours once you're inside.

▶ Download the museum's free app, either at home or using the on-site wi-fi. It offers several audio tours through the collection. Highlights, architecture and pop art are among the themes.

✗ **Take a Break**

The Gage (p36) cooks eclectic gastropub fare and pours whiskeys and beers to pair with it. The 1898 Berghoff (p38) is tops for a beer and a dose of Chicago history.

Top Sights
Willis Tower

For superlative seekers, Willis Tower is it: Chicago's tallest skyscraper, rising 1450ft into the heavens. Built in 1973 as the Sears Tower, the black-tubed behemoth reigned as the world's tallest building for almost 25 years. It still wins the prize for views from its 103rd-floor Skydeck, where glass-floored ledges jut out in midair and give a knee-buckling perspective straight down.

👁 Map p32, A4

www.theskydeck.com

233 S Wacker Dr

adult/child $23/15

🕙9am-10pm Mar-Sep, 10am-8pm Oct-Feb

Ⓜ Brown, Orange, Purple, Pink Line to Quincy

Facts & States

Before ascending, there are factoid-filled murals to ponder and a factoid-filled movie to watch. You'll learn about the 43,000 miles of phone cable used, the 2232 steps to the roof, and how the tower height is the equivalent of 313 Oprahs (or 262 Michael Jordans). Then it's time for the ear-popping, 70-second elevator ride to the top. From here, the entire city stretches below and you can see exactly how Chicago is laid out. On good days you can see for 40 to 50 miles, as far as Indiana, Michigan and Wisconsin. On hazy or stormy days you won't see much at all, so don't bother.

Ledges

The four ledges are on the deck's western side. They're like glass-encased boxes hanging out from the building's frame. If crowds are light, you can sprawl out on one for the ultimate photo op. If the ledges crack – which they did in 2014 when some folks stepped on them – fear not: that's not the glass cracking, but the protective coating covering the 1.5-inch-thick glass. You won't fall. Really. So don't even worry about it.

New Thrills

A new company recently bought the Willis Tower and announced plans to expand the Skydeck's features. Soon you might be able to rappel between the 103rd and 102nd floors inside a glass-enclosed box, or take a 'ledge walk' on a glass-pane balcony. Keep an eye on the sky here for more on the unnerving possibilities to come.

☑ Top Tips

▸ Avoid peak times in summer, between 11am and 4pm Friday to Sunday, when queues can surpass an hour.

▸ Buying tickets online saves some time, but there's a $2 surcharge per ticket.

▸ The entrance is on Jackson Blvd, where you go through security. The line to pay is down one level (staff will direct you there).

▸ Ask at the entrance and/or pay desk about visibility. Staff can call the Skydeck and provide updates.

✕ Take a Break

Grab a fat sandwich or red velvet cupcake made by culinary students at **Washburne Cafe** (www. washburneculinary.com; 226 W Jackson Blvd; mains $4-6; ⏱7:30am-3:30pm Mon-Fri). Global vegan dishes and organic wines feature at Native Foods Cafe (p37).

A

333 W Wacker Dr
W Lake St

B

N Franklin St
N Wells St

19

C

N LaSalle St
Clark/Lake M
N Clark St
James R Thompson Center
21

D

N Dearborn St
State/Lake M
N State St

1

W Randolph St

County Building & Chicago City Hall

Richard J Daley Center
Daley Plaza

Macy's (Marshall F Building.

2

South Branch Chicago River

N Wacker Dr

Washington/Wells M
W Washington St

Washington M

THE LOOP

23

W Calhoun Pl

E Calhoun Pl

W Madison St

Chase Building

3

S Wacker Dr

S Franklin St
W Monroe St
S Wells St
S LaSalle St
S Clark St
W Marble Pl
Monroe M
Mon
Monroe M
S State St

Willis Tower

W Adams St

Quincy M
Rookery
5
W Quincy St
14
11
Post Office

Chicago Federal Center

Chicago 17
Jackson M
Jackson M

4

Money Museum
6
W Jackson Blvd

Kluczynski Building

Chicago Board of Trade

S Financial Pl

26

H W Library

W Van Buren St

LaSalle/ Van Buren M

S Federal St
S Dearborn St

Harold Washington Library Center

5

LaSalle M

W Congress Pkwy

For reviews see

E
8 ⊙ ▲
Riverwalk
⊗12
E Lake St
N Wabash Ave
N Michigan Ave

F
N Stetson Ave

G
E Randolph St

H
Urban
Kayaks ⊙9 ▲
Lake Shore
East Park

Ⓝ 0 ———— 200 m
0 ———— 0.1 miles

Chicago -
Millennium
Station (Metra) 🚇

E Randolph St

Jay
Pritzker
Pavilion

4 ⊙ Bike
Chicago

E Randolph St

⊙ *Chicago*
1 *Cultural Center*

⭐24

Ⓜ E Washington St
🚇 18

Washington/
Wabash

Wrigley
Square

P ⭐20

Maggie Daley
Park

⊙3

AT&T
Plaza

*Millennium
Park*
⊙

Maggie
Daley
Park

N Columbus Dr

N Lake Shore Dr

E Madison St
13 ⊗   16 ⊗
10 ⊗

P

E Monroe St

P

E Monroe St

Butler
Field

Lakefront Trail

Ⓜ E Adams St
Route ⊙
66 Sign 7
22 ⭐
25 🏛

Adams/
Wabash

⊙ **Art Institute
of Chicago**

P

Petrillo
Music Shell

Lake Michigan

S Wabash Ave

E Jackson Blvd

Grant
Park

Van Buren St
🚇 (Metra)

S Columbus Dr

Grant Park

S Lake Shore Dr

E Van Buren St

15
⊗
E Congress Pkwy

*Buckingham
Fountain*
⊙2

Sights

Chicago Cultural Center
NOTABLE BUILDING

1 ◎ Map p32, E2

This exquisite, beaux-arts building began its life as the Chicago Public Library in 1897. Today the block-long building houses terrific art exhibitions (especially the 4th-floor Yates Gallery), as well as jazz and classical concerts at lunchtime (12:15pm most Mondays and every Wednesday). It also contains the world's largest Tiffany stained-glass dome, on the 3rd floor where the library circulation desk used to be. InstaGreeter (p146) tours of the Loop depart from the Randolph St lobby, as do Millennium Park tours. And it's all free! (☏312-744-6630; www.chicagoculturalcenter.org; 78 E Washington St; admission free; ⏱9am-7pm Mon-Thu, to 6pm Fri & Sat, 10am-6pm Sun;

M Brown, Orange, Green, Purple, Pink Line to Washington/Wabash)

Buckingham Fountain
FOUNTAIN

2 ◎ Map p32, G5

Grant Park's centerpiece is one of the world's largest fountains, with a 1.5-million-gallon capacity and a 15-story-high spray. It lets loose on the hour from 8am to 11pm early May to mid-October, accompanied at night by multicolored lights and music. (301 S Columbus Dr; M Red Line to Harrison)

Maggie Daley Park
PARK

3 ◎ Map p32, G2

Families love this park's fanciful free playgrounds in all their enchanted-forest and pirate-themed glory. There's also a rock-climbing wall, 18-hole mini-golf course, in-line skating ribbon (which becomes an ice-skating ribbon in winter) and tennis courts; these features have fees. Multiple picnic tables make the park an excellent spot to relax. It connects to Millennium Park via the pedestrian BP Bridge (p26). (www.maggiedaleypark.com; 337 E Randolph St; ⏱6am-11pm; 👶; M Brown, Orange, Green, Purple, Pink Line to Washington/Wabash)

Bike Chicago
CYCLING

4 ◎ Map p32, G2

Rent a bike to explore DIY-style, or go on a guided tour. Tours cover themes such as lakefront parks and attractions, breweries and historic neighborhoods, or downtown's sights and fireworks at

---

○ Local Life
Daley Plaza

A peculiar Picasso sculpture marks the heart of **Daley Plaza** (Map p32, C2; 50 W Washington St; M Blue Line to Washington). It's the place to be come lunchtime, particularly when the weather warms up. You never know what will be going on – dance performances, bands, ethnic festivals, holiday celebrations – but you do know it'll be free. A farmers market sets up on Thursday (7am to 3pm) from April through October.

JAMES KIRKIKIS/SHUTTERSTOCK ©

Atrium at the Chicago Cultural Center

night (highly recommended). Prices include lock, helmet and map. This main branch operates out of the McDonald's Cycle Center (p26) in Millennium Park; there's another branch on Navy Pier. (☑312-729-1000; www.bikechicago.com; 239 E Randolph St; bikes per hour/day from $9/30; ☺6:30am-10pm Mon-Fri, from 8am Sat & Sun Jun-Aug, reduced hours rest of year; MⒷBrown, Orange, Green, Purple, Pink Line to Washington/Wabash)

Rookery ARCHITECTURE

5 ◉ Map p32, C4

The famed firm of Burnham and Root built the Rookery in 1888 and Frank Lloyd Wright remodeled the atrium 19 years later. It's renowned because while it looks hulking and fortress-like outside, it's light and airy inside. You can walk in and look around for free. Tours ($10 to $15) are available weekdays at 11am, noon and 1pm. (☑312-994-4000; www.flwright.org; 209 S LaSalle St; ☺9am-5pm Mon-Fri; MⒷBrown, Orange, Purple, Pink Line to Quincy)

Money Museum MUSEUM

6 ◉ Map p32, B4

This small museum in the Federal Reserve Bank of Chicago is fun for a quick browse. The best exhibits include a giant glass cube stuffed with one million $1 bills (they weigh 2000lb) and a counterfeit display differentiating real bills from fakes.

Learn why we call $1000 a 'grand,' and snap a sweet photo clutching the million-dollar-stuffed briefcase. (☑312-322-2400; www.chicagofed.org; 230 S LaSalle St; admission free; ☺8:30am-5pm Mon-Fri; ⓜBrown, Orange, Purple, Pink Line to Quincy)

Route 66 Sign
HISTORIC SITE

 Map p32, E4

Attention Route 66 buffs: the Mother Road's starting point is here. Look for the 'Historic 66 Begin' sign that marks the spot on Adams St's southern side as you head west toward Wabash Ave. There are a couple of other 66 signs on the same block, but this one is the original. (E Adams St, btwn S Michigan & Wabash Aves; ⓜBrown, Orange, Green, Purple, Pink Line to Adams)

Riverwalk
WATERFRONT

 Map p32, E1

Clasping the Chicago River's southern side along Wacker Dr, this 1.5-mile-long promenade is a fine spot to escape the crowds and watch boats glide by.

Top Tip

Pack a Picnic

Pack a picnic and meander over to Millennium Park (Map p32, E2; p24) to hear a free concert. Indie rock, world music or classical performers take the stage nightly in summer, including many big-name musicians. Pastoral (p37) and Toni Patisserie (p38) can set you up with deli goods and wine.

Access it from the stairs at any bridge. Outdoor cafes, umbrella-shaded bars, a kayak rental shop and a fountain you can splash in dot the way. The broad steps between Clark and LaSalle Sts offer a good refuge to sit and relax. (www.chicagoriverwalk.us; Chicago River waterfront along Wacker Dr, btwn N Lake Shore Dr & W Lake St; ⓜBrown, Orange, Green, Purple, Pink, Blue Line to State/Lake)

Urban Kayaks
KAYAKING

 Map p32, H1

Located on the Riverwalk, this outfitter rents kayaks for Chicago River explorations; experience is required to head out on your own. The company also offers guided tours that glide past downtown's skyscrapers and historic sites; beginners are welcome, as each tour begins with a 20-minute training session. For extra help, the company offers an hour-long 'intro to paddling' class ($45). (☑312-965-0035; www.urbankayaks.com; 435 E Riverwalk S; per hour $30, tours $55-80; ☺9am-5pm Mon-Fri, to 6pm Sat & Sun May-early Oct; ⓜBrown, Orange, Green, Purple, Pink Line to State/Lake)

Eating

Gage
GASTROPUB $$$

 Map p32, E3

This always-hopping gastropub dishes up fanciful grub, from Gouda-topped venison burgers to mussels vindaloo or Guinness-battered fish and chips. The booze rocks too, including a solid whiskey list and small-batch beers that pair with the food. (📞312-372-4243; www.thegage chicago.com; 24 S Michigan Ave; mains $18-36; ⏰11am-9pm Mon, to 11pm Tue-Thu, to midnight Fri, 10am-midnight Sat, 10am-10pm Sun; Ⓜ️Brown, Orange, Green, Purple, Pink Line to Washington/Wabash)

Revival Food Hall
AMERICAN $

11 Map p32, C4

The Loop has craved a forward-thinking food court for ages. Which is why, come lunchtime, hipster office workers pack the blond wood tables at Revival Food Hall, the modern, lantern-adorned marketplace on the ground floor of the historic National building. The all-local dining concept brings some of Chicago's best fast-casual food to the masses, from Antique Taco and Smoque BBQ to Furious Spoon ramen. (📞773-999-9411; www.revivalfoodhall.com; 125 S Clark St; mains $7-12; ⏰7am-7pm Mon-Fri; Ⓜ️Blue Line to Monroe)

Pastoral
DELI $

12 Map p32, E1

Pastoral makes a mean sandwich. Fresh-shaved serrano ham, Basque salami and other carnivorous fixings meet smoky mozzarella, Gruyère and piquant spreads slathered on crusty baguettes. Vegetarians also have options. There's limited seating; most folks take away for picnics in Millennium Park (call in your order a few hours in advance to avoid a queue). The shop sells bottles of beer and wine too. (📞312-658-

1250; www.pastoralartisan.com; 53 E Lake St; sandwiches $8-12; ⏰10:30am-8pm Mon-Fri, 11am-6pm Sat & Sun; 🚴; Ⓜ️Brown, Orange, Green, Purple, Pink Line to Randolph or State/Lake)

Pizano's
PIZZA $

13 Map p32, E3

Pizano's is a good recommendation for deep-dish newbies, since it's not jaw-breakingly thick. The thin-crust pies that hit the checker-clothed tables are good too, winning rave reviews for crispness. Some of the wait staff are characters who've been around forever, which adds to the convivial ambience. It's open late-night (with a full bar), which is a Loop rarity. (📞312-236-1777; www.pizanoschicago.com; 61 E Madison St; small pizzas from $16; ⏰11am-2am Sun-Fri, to 3am Sat; 📶; Ⓜ️Red, Blue Line to Monroe)

Native Foods Cafe
VEGAN $

14 Map p32, C4

If you're looking for vegan fast-casual fare downtown, Native Foods is your spot. The meatball sandwich rocks the seitan, while the scorpion burger fires up hot-spiced tempeh. Local beers and organic wines accompany the wide-ranging menu of Greek-, Asian-, Mexican- and Italian-inspired dishes. Soy-free, gluten-free and nut-free menus are available for allergy sufferers. (📞312-332-6332; www.nativefoods.com; 218 S Clark St; mains $9-11; ⏰10:30am-9pm Mon-Sat, 11am-7pm Sun; 🚴; Ⓜ️Brown, Orange, Purple, Pink Line to Quincy)

Cafecito
CUBAN $

15 Map p32, E5

Attached to the HI-Chicago hostel and perfect for the hungry, thrifty traveler, Cafecito serves killer Cuban sandwiches layered with citrus-garlic-marinated roasted pork and ham. Strong coffee and hearty egg sandwiches make a fine breakfast. (☏312-922-2233; www.cafecitochicago.com; 26 E Congress Pkwy; mains $6-10; ☺7am-9pm Mon-Fri, 10am-6pm Sat & Sun; ☐; Ⓜ Brown, Orange, Purple, Pink Line to Library)

Shake Shack
BURGERS $

16 Map p32, E3

This burger chain is beloved for its well-griddled patties under a sweet-and-tangy Shake Sauce, crinkle-cut fries and milkshakes made with creamy custard (with local doughnuts and pie blended in). Are the shakes really the nation's best? The endless crowd of happy slurpers provides the answer. (☏312-646-6005; www.shakeshack.com; 12 S Michigan Ave; mains $6-10; ☺11am-11pm; Ⓜ Brown, Orange, Green, Purple, Pink Line to Washington/Wabash)

Drinking

Berghoff
BAR

17 Map p32, D4

The Berghoff dates from 1898 and was the first spot in town to serve a legal drink after Prohibition (ask to see the liquor license stamped '#1'). Little has changed around the antique wood bar since then. Belly up for frosty mugs of the house-brand beer and order sauerbraten, schnitzel and other old-world classics from the adjoining German restaurant. (☏312-427-3170; www.theberghoff.com; 17 W Adams St; ☺11am-9pm Mon-Fri, 11:30am-9pm Sat; Ⓜ Blue, Red Line to Jackson)

Toni Patisserie & Cafe
CAFE

18 Map p32, E2

Toni's provides a cute refuge for a glass of wine. The Parisian-style cafe has a small list of French red, white and sparkling wines to sip at the close-set tables while you try to resist the éclairs, macaroons and tiered cakes tempting from the glass case. It also sells bottles for take away (handy for park picnics). (☏312-726-2020; www.tonipatisserie.com; 65 E Washington St; ☺7am-7pm Mon-Fri, 8am-7pm Sat, 9am-5pm Sun; Ⓜ Brown, Orange, Green, Purple, Pink Line to Washington/Wabash)

Monk's Pub
PUB

19 Map p32, B1

Grab the brass handles on the huge wooden doors and enter this dimly lit Belgian beer cave. Old barrels, vintage taps and faux antiquarian books set the mood, accompanied by a whopping international brew selection and free, throw-your-shells-on-the-floor peanuts. Office workers and the occasional TV weather presenter are the main folks hanging out at Monk's, which also serves good, burger-y pub grub. (☏312-357-6665; www.monkspubchicago.com; 205 W Lake St; ☺9am-11pm

Mon-Fri, 11am-5pm Sat; Blue, Brown, Orange, Green, Purple, Pink Line to Clark/Lake)

Cindy's
BAR

Cindy's (see 17 Map p32, E3) unfurls awesome views of Millennium Park and the lake from atop the Chicago Athletic Association Hotel. Sit at one of the long wood tables under twinkling lights and sip snazzy cocktails with ingredients such as mugolio pine sap. Alas, everyone wants in on the action, so try to come early to avoid having to wait for a seat. (☎312-792-3502; www.cindysrooftop.com; 12 S Michigan Ave; ⏰11am-1am Mon-Fri, 10am-2am Sat, to midnight Sun; Brown, Orange, Green, Purple, Pink Line to Washington/Wabash)

Entertainment

Grant Park Orchestra
CLASSICAL MUSIC

20 ⭐ Map p32, F2

It's a summertime must-do. The Grant Park Orchestra – composed of top-notch musicians from symphonies worldwide – puts on free classical concerts at Millennium Park's Pritzker Pavilion (p25). Patrons bring lawn chairs, blankets, wine and picnic fixings to set the scene as the sun dips, the skyscraper lights flicker on and glorious music fills the night air. (☎312-742-7638; www.grantparkmusicfestival.com; Pritzker Pavilion, Millennium Park; ⏰6:30pm Wed & Fri, 7:30pm Sat mid-Jun–mid-Aug;

Top Tip

Photo Op

What's more perfect for your Chicago selfie backdrop than a six-story-high sign spelling the city's name in bright, glittering lights? The eye-popper in front of the **Chicago Theatre** (Map p 32, D1; ☎312-462-6300; www.thechicagotheatre.com; 175 N State St; Brown, Orange, Green, Purple, Pink Line to State/Lake) is an official landmark and sets the scene flawlessly.

Brown, Orange, Green, Purple, Pink Line to Washington/Wabash)

Goodman Theatre
THEATER

21 ⭐ Map p32, D1

This is one of Chicago's premier drama houses, and its Theater District facility is gorgeous. It specializes in new and classic American productions and has been cited several times as one of the USA's best regional theaters. At 10am Goodman puts unsold tickets for the current day's performance on sale for half-price online; they're also available at the box office from noon. (☎312-443-3800; www.goodmantheatre.org; 170 N Dearborn St; Brown, Orange, Green, Purple, Pink, Blue Line to Clark/Lake)

Chicago Symphony Orchestra
CLASSICAL MUSIC

22 ⭐ Map p32, E4

Riccardo Muti leads the CSO, one of America's best symphonies, known

Understand
Chicago Architecture

First Chicago School (1872–99)
Though the 1871 fire didn't seem like an opportunity at the time, it made Chicago what it is today. The chance to reshape the city's burned downtown drew young, ambitious architects including Dankmar Adler, Daniel Burnham, John Root and Louis Sullivan. These men and their colleagues made up the First Chicago School (some say they practiced the Commercial style), which stressed economy, simplicity and function. Using steel frames and elevators, their pinnacle achievement was the modern skyscraper. The Rookery (p35) is a good example of the genre.

Prairie School (1895–1915) & Beaux Arts (1893–1920)
Frank Lloyd Wright, a protégé of Louis Sullivan, endowed Chicago with its most distinctive style, the Prairie School. Wright's designs reflected the Midwest's landscape – low-slung, with long horizontal lines and lots of earth colors. Robie House (p125) is his Prairie masterwork.

While the First Chicago School and Prairie School were forward-looking inventions, beaux arts took after a French fad that stressed antiquity. The popularity of the style was spurred on by the colossal French neoclassical structures of Daniel Burnham's 'White City,' built for the 1893 World's Exposition. Beaux-arts examples include the Museum of Science & Industry (p125) and Chicago Cultural Center (p34).

Second Chicago School (1946–79) & Skyscrapers Today
Ludwig Mies van der Rohe made sure the city stayed at the forefront of innovation in the 1950s. With his tools of exposed metal and glass, along with a less-is-more creed, he pioneered the Second Chicago School style of architecture. The Loop's **Kluczynski Federal Building** (230 S Dearborn St; M Blue Line to Jackson) shows how it's done.

The local architects of Skidmore, Owings & Merrill further developed Mies' ideas, and stretched the modern skyscraper even higher with the John Hancock Center and Sears (now Willis) Tower (p30). The latter remained the world's tallest building for almost a quarter century. Today Chicago continues to push the boundaries of modern design with cloud toppers such as Jeanne Gang's wavy **Aqua Tower** (225 N Columbus Dr; M Brown, Orange, Green, Purple, Pink Line to State/Lake).

for fervent subscribers and an untouchable brass section. Cellist Yo-Yo Ma is the group's creative consultant and a frequent soloist. The season runs from September to May at Symphony Center; Daniel Burnham designed the Orchestra Hall. (☎312-294-3000; www.cso.org; 220 S Michigan Ave; Ⓜ Brown, Orange, Green, Purple, Pink Line to Adams)

Lyric Opera of Chicago   OPERA

23 ⭐ Map p32, A2

Tickets are hard to come by for this bold modern opera company, which fills the chandeliered Civic Opera House with a shrewd mix of common classics and daring premieres from September to March. If your Italian isn't up to much, don't be put off; much to the horror of purists, the company projects English 'supertitles' above the proscenium. (☎312-332-2244; www.lyricopera.org; 20 N Wacker Dr; Ⓜ Brown, Orange, Purple, Pink Line to Washington/Wells)

Hubbard Street Dance Chicago   DANCE

24 ⭐ Map p32, F2

Hubbard Street is the pre-eminent dance company in the city, with a well-deserved international reputation to match. The group is known for energetic and technically virtuosic performances under the direction of some of the best choreographers in the world. It performs at the Harris Theater in Millennium Park. (☎312-850-9744; www.hubbardstreetdance.com; 205 E Randolph St; Ⓜ Brown, Orange, Green, Purple, Pink Line to Washington/Wabash)

Shopping

Chicago Architecture Foundation Shop   GIFTS & SOUVENIRS

25 🅰 Map p32, E4

Skyline posters, Frank Lloyd Wright note cards, skyscraper models and heaps of books celebrate local architecture at this haven for anyone with an edifice complex. The items make excellent only-in-Chicago-type souvenirs. (☎312-322-1132; www.architecture.org/shop; 224 S Michigan Ave; ⏰9am-9pm, shorter hours in winter; Ⓜ Brown, Orange, Green, Purple, Pink Line to Adams)

Optimo Hats   FASHION & ACCESSORIES

26 🅰 Map p32, D4

Optimo is a Chicago institution, the last custom hat-maker for men in town. Want a lid like Capone? Get one here, made with serious, old-school craftsmanship. Clients include Johnny Depp, Jack White and a slew of local bluesmen. The shop is located in the landmark **Monadnock Building**. (www.monadnockbuilding.com; 53 W Jackson Blvd; www.optimo.com; 51 W Jackson Blvd; ⏰10am-5pm Mon-Sat; Ⓜ Blue Line to Jackson)

Explore

Near North & Navy Pier

The Near North packs in deep-dish pizza parlors, buzzy bistros, art galleries and so many upscale stores that its main vein – Michigan Ave – has been dubbed the 'Magnificent Mile.' Bulging out to the east is Navy Pier, a half-mile-long wharf of tour boats, carnival rides and a flashy, king-sized Ferris wheel. Both areas bustle day and night.

The Sights in a Day

☼ Have breakfast at **Doughnut Vault** (p50), munching fluffy glazed goodies, or **Xoco** (p50), gobbling the rich churros. Walk along the **Magnificent Mile** (p48) and ogle the architecture of the **Tribune Tower** (p48) in between shopping stops. Resistance is futile: give in to the heavenly smell and buy a bag of **Garrett Popcorn** (p52).

☼ Make your way east to **Navy Pier** (p44). Don't be a sissy: get on the Ferris wheel for killer views of the city. Or rent a bike from **Bobby's Bike Hike** (p48) and head out on the Lakefront Trail. After all the exercise, you've earned a drink at **Clark Street Ale House** (p51) or **Arbella** (p51).

☾ Sup on swine and wine with the crowds at **Purple Pig** (p50) or open wide for deep-dish pizza with the masses at **Giordano's** (p50). Later, jazz fans can settle in at **Andy's** (p52), while blues fans can do the same at **Blue Chicago** (p52).

⊙ Top Sight
Navy Pier (p44)

♥ Best of Chicago

Architecture
Tribune Tower (p48)

Marina City (p48)

Eating
Xoco (p50)

Giordano's (p50)

Drinking
Arbella (p51)

Sports & Activities
Bobby's Bike Hike (p48)

For Kids
Chicago Children's Museum (p49)

Navy Pier (p44)

Shopping
Garrett Popcorn (p52)

Getting There

Ⓜ **El** Red Line to Grand for the Magnificent Mile's southern end; Red Line to Chicago for the Mag Mile's northern end; Brown, Purple Line to Chicago for River North.

🚎 **Trolley** A free trolley runs from the Red Line Grand stop to Navy Pier from late May to early September.

Top Sights
Navy Pier

Navy Pier was once the city's municipal wharf. Today it's one of Chicago's most visited attractions, with eight million people per year flooding its half-mile length. Locals may groan about its commercialization, but even they can't refute the brilliant lakefront views, cool breezes and whopping fireworks displays in summer. Kids go gaga over the high-tech rides, fast-food restaurants and trinket vendors.

⊙ Map p46, H3

600 E Grand Ave

admission free

🕓 10am-10pm Sun-Thu, to midnight Fri & Sat Jun-Aug, 10am-8pm Sun-Thu, to 10pm Fri & Sat Sep-May

Ⓜ Red Line to Grand

Centennial Wheel & Other Rides

No visit to the pier is complete without a stomach-curdling turn on the gigantic, 196ft-tall **Centennial Wheel** (adult/child $15/12), which unfurls great views. The **carousel** (per ride $5; ☺May-Oct) is a beloved kiddie classic, with bobbing carved horses and organ music. There's also a giant swing that spins you out over the pier. Each attraction costs $6 to $15. For young ones in need of further amusements, the Chicago Children's Museum (p49) is on the pier near the main entrance.

Theaters & Tour Boats

An **IMAX Theater** (☎312-595-5629; www.imax.com; tickets $15-22) and the Chicago Shakespeare Theater (p52) also call the pier home. Keep an eye on the glistening white-canopied 'tent': the Shakespeare Theater recently converted it into a kicky additional venue for its populist takes on the Bard. Competing tour boats depart from the pier's southern side, where you can set sail in everything from a tall-masted schooner to thrill-ride speedboat. The splashy fountain by the pier's entrance entertains with lights and dancing spouts; it's being developed to convert into an ice rink in winter.

Past & Future

Navy Pier opened in 1916. During the past century it has seen action as a busy inland port, a WWII Navy pilot training center, a university campus, a convention center and now an entertainment complex. It has had a reputation in recent years as being tacky, but the city is trying to change that. A multimillion-dollar renovation is bringing more performance spaces, upgraded eating and drinking options, a hotel and more through 2018.

☑ Top Tips

▶ Crowds amass for the summer fireworks shows on Wednesday at 9:30pm and Saturday at 10:15pm.

▶ In summer the Shoreline water taxi (adult/child $8/4 Sunday through Friday, $10/5 Saturday) glides from Navy Pier to the Museum Campus, offering a fun alternative to land-based transport.

▶ Vendors sell beer and alcohol from walk-up windows, so you can stroll and drink on the pier.

✗ Take a Break

Heft a gargantuan slice of stuffed pizza at the pier outpost of **Giordano's** (☎312-288-8783; www.giordanos.com; 700 E Grand Ave; small pizzas from $16.50; ☺10am-9pm Sun-Thu, to 10pm Fri & Sat). Seek out **Original Rainbow Cone**, in a kiosk halfway down the pier on the south side (where all the boats line up). A scoop is actually five 'slices' of different flavored ice cream.

A

B

C   GOLD COAST

D

W Locust St

W Delaware Pl

Washington Square

W Delaware Pl

E Delaware Pl

John Hancock Center

1

W Chestnut St

W Tooker Pl

E Chestnut St

Water Tower Place

W Institute Pl

W Chestnut St

Chicago

Chicago

W Chicago Ave

16

Chicago

E Chicago Ave

RIVER NORTH GALLERY DISTRICT

NEAR NORTH

8

14

W Superior St

2

13

W Huron St

Driehaus Museum

5

1

W Erie St

(Magnificent Mile)

W Ontario St

Magnificent Mile

20

3

W Ohio St

15 18

Grand

12

W Grand Ave

N Michigan Ave

W Illinois St

10

E Illinois

W Hubbard St

9

11

Tribune Tower

Richard Norton Gallery

17

E Hubbard St

7

W Kinzie St

E Kinzie St

4

Merchandise Mart

Marina City

Trump Tower

3

ILLINOIS CENTER

W Wacker Dr

E Wacker Pl

N Wacker Dr

Clark/Lake

5

W Lake St

State/Lake

N Michigan Ave

Penton Pl

N Mies van der Rohe Way

N Dewitt Pl

E Pearson St

N Lake Shore Dr

Lakefront Trail

eneca Park

Lake Shore Park

Superior St

Northwestern University Chicago Campus

N Lake Shore Dr

Huron St

N Fairbanks Ct

E Erie St

Ohio Street Beach

Olive Park

Water Filtration Plant

STREETERVILLE

E Ontario St

N McClurg Ct

E Ohio St

E Grand Ave

Bobby's Bike Hike ◎ 4

NAVY PIER

Chicago Children's Museum ◎ 6

P

E Illinois St

Navy Pier ◉

19 ✦

City ront Plaza

Ogden Plaza

N New St

N McClurg Ct

E North Water St

River Esplanade

Chicago River

Hyatt egency hicago

N Columbus Dr

E Wacker Dr

N Lake Shore Dr

Lakefront Trail

Lake Michigan

Lake Shore East Park

Harbor Dr

Sights

Magnificent Mile   AREA

1 ⦿ Map p46, D3

Spanning Michigan Ave between the river and Oak St, the Mag Mile is Chicago's much-touted upscale shopping strip, where Bloomingdale's, Apple, Burberry and many more will lighten your wallet. The retailers are mostly high-end chains that have stores nationwide. (www.themagnificentmile.com; N Michigan Ave; Ⓜ Red Line to Grand)

Tribune Tower   ARCHITECTURE

2 ⦿ Map p46, D4

Take a close look when passing by this 1925 neo-Gothic edifice. Colonel Robert McCormick, eccentric owner of the *Chicago Tribune* in the early 1900s, collected – and asked his reporters to send – rocks from famous buildings and monuments around the world. He stockpiled pieces of the Taj Mahal, Westminster Abbey, the Great Pyramid and more than 140 others, which are now lodged around the tower's base. (435 N Michigan Ave; Ⓜ Red Line to Grand)

Marina City   ARCHITECTURE

3 ⦿ Map p46, C4

For bit of fun, check out the twin corncob towers of the 1964 Marina City. Bertrand Goldberg designed the futuristic high-rise, and it has become an iconic part of the Chicago skyline (check out the cover of the Wilco CD *Yankee Hotel Foxtrot*). And yes, there is a marina at the towers' base. (300 N State St; Ⓜ Brown, Orange, Green, Purple, Pink Line to State/Lake)

Bobby's Bike Hike   CYCLING

4 ⦿ Map p46, G3

Locally based Bobby's earns rave reviews from riders. It rents bikes and has easy access to the Lakefront Trail. It also offers cool tours ($35 to $66) of South Side gangster sites, the lakefront, nighttime vistas, and venues to indulge in pizza and beer. The Tike Hike caters to kids. Enter through the covered driveway to reach the shop. (☏ 312-245-9300; www.bobbysbikehike.com; 540 N Lake Shore Dr; per hour/day from $10/34; ⊘ 8:30am-8pm Mon-Fri, 8am-8pm Sat & Sun Jun-Aug, 9am-7pm Mar-May & Sep-Nov; Ⓜ Red Line to Grand)

Driehaus Museum   MUSEUM

5 ⦿ Map p46, C2

Set in the exquisite Nickerson Mansion, the Driehaus immerses visitors in Gilded Age decorative arts and architecture. You'll feel like a *Great Gatsby* character as you wander three floors stuffed with sumptuous objets d'art and stained glass. Recommended guided tours ($5 extra) are available four times daily. The price seems steep, but the museum is a prize for those intrigued by opulent interiors. (☏ 312-482-8933; www.driehausmuseum.org; 40 E Erie St; adult/

FRASER HALL/GETTY IMAGES ©

Magnificent Mile

child $20/10; ⊘10am-5pm Tue-Sun; Ⓜ Red Line to Chicago)

Chicago Children's Museum MUSEUM

6 ◉ Map p46, H3

Designed to challenge the imaginations of toddlers to 10-year-olds, this colorful museum near Navy Pier's main entrance gives young visitors enough hands-on exhibits to keep them climbing and creating for hours. Among the favorites, Dinosaur Expedition explores the world of paleontology and lets kids excavate 'bones.' They can also climb a ropey schooner; bowl in a faux alley; get wet in the waterways (and learn about hydroelectric power); and use real tools to build things in the Tinkering Lab. (☎312-527-1000; www.chicagochildrensmuseum.org; 700 E Grand Ave; admission $14; ⊘10am-5pm, to 8pm Thu; 🚼; Ⓜ Red Line to Grand)

Richard Norton Gallery GALLERY

7 ◉ Map p46, A4

Located in the Merchandise Mart, this gallery specializes in impressionist, modernist and historical Chicago-focused works. Check out the early beach and street scenes of the city. (☎312-644-8855; www.richardnortongallery.com; 222 W Merchandise Mart Plaza, Ste 612; ⊘9am-5pm Mon-Fri; Ⓜ Brown, Purple Line to Merchandise Mart)

Eating

Giordano's
PIZZA $$

8 Map p46, D2

Giordano's makes 'stuffed' pizza, a bigger, doughier version of deep dish. It's awesome. If you want a slice of heaven, order the 'special,' a stuffed pie containing sausage, mushroom, green pepper and onions. Each pizza takes 45 minutes to bake. (☏312-951-0747; www.giordanos.com; 730 N Rush St; small pizzas from $16.50; ⏱11am-11pm Sun-Thu, to midnight Fri & Sat; Ⓜ Red Line to Chicago)

Xoco
MEXICAN $

9 Map p46, B4

At celeb-chef Rick Bayless' Mexican street-food restaurant (pronounced '*show*-co') everything is sourced from local small farms. Crunch into warm churros (spiraled dough fritters) with

Local Life
Doughnut Vault

The chandelier-clad **Doughnut Vault** (Map p46, A4; www.doughnutvault.com; 401 N Franklin St; doughnuts $2.25-3.50; ⏱8am-3pm Mon-Fri, 9:30am-3pm Sat & Sun; Ⓜ Brown, Purple Line to Merchandise Mart) is indeed in a vault – an old bank vault – with room for only a handful of people. The glazed doughnuts (vanilla or chestnut) are the beauties here, giant and fluffy as a pillow. The shop usually sells out before closing time, so check Twitter (@doughnutvault) beforehand.

chili-spiked hot chocolate for breakfast, crusty *tortas* (sandwiches, such as the succulent mushroom and goat cheese) for lunch and *caldos* (meal-in-a-bowl soups) for dinner. Queues can be long; breakfast is the least crowded time. (www.rickbayless.com; 449 N Clark St; mains $9-14; ⏱8am-9pm Tue-Thu, to 10pm Fri & Sat; Ⓜ Red Line to Grand)

Purple Pig
MEDITERRANEAN $$

10 Map p46, D3

The Pig's Magnificent Mile location, wide-ranging meat and veggie menu, and late-night serving hours make it a crowd-pleaser. Milk-braised pork shoulder is the hamtastic specialty. Dishes are meant to be shared, and the long list of affordable vinos gets the good times rolling at communal tables both indoors and out. Alas, there are no reservations to help beat the crowds. (☏312-464-1744; www.thepurplepigchicago.com; 500 N Michigan Ave; small plates $10-20; ⏱11:30am-midnight Sun-Thu, to 1am Fri & Sat; ✷; Ⓜ Red Line to Grand)

Billy Goat Tavern
BURGERS $

11 Map p46, D4

Tribune and *Sun Times* reporters have guzzled in the subterranean Billy Goat for decades. Order a 'cheezborger' and Schlitz beer, then look around at the newspapered walls to get the scoop on infamous local stories. The place is a tourist magnet, but a deserving one. Follow the tavern signs that lead below Michigan Ave to get here. Cash only. (☏312-222-1525; www.billygoattavern.com; lower level, 430 N Michigan Ave; burgers $4-8;

6am-1am Mon-Thu, to 2am Fri, to 3am Sat, 9am-2am Sun; M Red Line to Grand)

Eataly
ITALIAN $$

12 Map p46, C3

This two-story food emporium overwhelms when you step inside. The winners among the many restaurants and cafe stations strewn throughout include La Focaccia (warm, bread-y goodness), Nutella (spread thick on bread or in crepes) and the Birreria (suds brewed on site). Can't decide? Hit the wine bar (2nd floor) for a takeaway glass and then sip as you wander the premises to choose. (312-521-8700; www.eataly.com; 43 E Ohio St; snack items $4-13, mains $14-25; 10am-11pm; M Red Line to Grand)

Mr Beef
SANDWICHES $

13 Map p46, A2

It's a classic for the local Italian beef sandwich specialty. It arrives on a long, spongy white bun that begins dribbling (that's a good thing!) after a load of the spicy meat and cooking juices has been ladled on. The *giardiniera* (spicy pickled vegetables) adds heat. Don't be afraid of the dumpy decor. Cash only. (312-337-8500; www.facebook.com/mrbeefchicago; 666 N Orleans St; sandwiches $6-9; 10am-6pm Mon-Thu, to 5am Fri & Sat; M Brown, Purple Line to Chicago)

Gino's East
PIZZA $$

14 Map p46, D2

In the deep-dish pizza wars, Gino's is easily one of the top-five heavies. And it

encourages customers to do something wacky: cover every available surface – walls, chairs, staircases – with graffiti. The classic cheese-and-sausage pie oozes countless pounds of gooey goodness over a crispy golden crust. Prepare to wait for the pleasure as reservations are not accepted. (312-266-3337; www.ginoseast.com; 162 E Superior St; small pizzas from $18; 11am-9pm Sun-Thu, to 10pm Fri & Sat; M Red Line to Chicago)

Drinking

Arbella
COCKTAIL BAR

15 Map p46, B3

Named for a 17th-century ship full of wine-guzzling passengers, Arbella is an adventuresome cocktail bar. Booze from around the globe makes its way into the drinks, from rye to rum, pisco to mezcal. Park yourself at a dark leather banquette, under sparkly globe lights, and taste-trip the night away in one of the city's coziest rooms. (312-846-6654; www.arbellachicago.com; 112 W Grand Ave; 5pm-midnight Sun & Mon, to 2am Thu & Fri, to 3am Sat; M Red Line to Grand)

Clark Street Ale House
BAR

16 Map p46, B2

Do as the retro sign advises and 'Stop & Drink.' Midwestern microbrews are the main draw. Work up a thirst on the free pretzels, order a three-beer sampler for $7 and cool off in the beer garden out back. (312-642-9253; www.clarkstreetalehouse.com; 742 N Clark St;

⏱4pm–4am Mon-Fri, from 11am Sat & Sun; 📶; Ⓜ Red Line to Chicago)

Entertainment

Andy's

JAZZ

17 ⭐ Map p46, C4

This comfy jazz club programs a far-ranging lineup of local traditional, swing, bop, Latin, fusion and Afro-pop acts, along with the occasional big-name performer. It has been on the scene for several years, and its downtown location makes it a popular spot for post-work boppers. (📞312-642-6805; www.andysjazzclub.com; 11 E Hubbard St; cover $10-15; ⏱4pm-1:30am; Ⓜ Red Line to Grand)

Blue Chicago

BLUES

18 ⭐ Map p46, B3

If you're staying in the neighborhood and don't feel like hitting the road, you won't go wrong at this main-stream blues club. Commanding local acts wither the mics nightly. (📞312-661-0100; www.bluechicago.com; 536 N Clark St; cover $10-12; ⏱8pm-1:30am Sun-Fri, to 2:30am Sat; Ⓜ Red Line to Grand)

Chicago Shakespeare Theater

THEATER

19 ⭐ Map p46, H3

Snuggled into a beautiful glass home on Navy Pier, this company is at the top of its game, presenting works from the Bard that are fresh, inventive and timeless. In summer the group puts on Shakespeare in the Parks – free performances of one of Will's classics that travel to more than a dozen neighborhoods. Take the trolley from Grand. (📞312-595-5600; www.chicagoshakes.com; 800 E Grand Ave; Ⓜ Red Line to Grand)

Shopping

Garrett Popcorn

FOOD

20 🔒 Map p46, D3

Like lemmings drawn to a cliff, people form long lines outside this store on the Mag Mile. Granted, the caramel corn is heavenly and the cheese popcorn decadent, but is it worth waiting in the whipping snow for a chance to buy some? Actually, it is. Buy the Garrett Mix, which combines the two flavors. The entrance is on Ontario St. (📞312-944-2630; www.garrettpopcorn.com; 625 N Michigan Ave; ⏱10am-8pm Mon-Thu, to 10pm Fri & Sat, to 7pm Sun; Ⓜ Red Line to Grand)

Local Life
Green Door Tavern

The **Green Door Tavern** (Map p46, A2; 📞312-664-5496; www.greendoorchicago.com; 678 N Orleans St; mains $10-18; ⏱11:30am-2am Mon-Fri, 10am-2am Sat & Sun; 📶; Ⓜ Brown, Purple Line to Chicago), tucked in an 1872 building, is your place to mingle with locals amid old photos and memorabilia. During Prohibition years, a door painted green meant there was a speakeasy in the basement. It's still there and now holds a small cocktail bar.

Understand
Al Capone
- -

Early Days
Alphonse Gabriel Capone was born in New York City in 1899. He moved to Chicago 20 years later, encouraged by his gangster mentor Johnny Torrio, who promised a city of opportunity. Capone quickly moved up the local ranks and became the mob boss in 1924, taking control of the city's South Side and expanding his empire by making 'hits' on his rivals. Capone typically sent his submachine-gun-toting lieutenants to carry out these bloody acts. Incidentally, Capone earned the nickname 'Scarface' not because he ended up on the wrong side of a bullet but because a dance-hall fight left him with a large scar on his left cheek.

Success & Downfall
Prohibition fueled the success of the Chicago mob. Not surprisingly, the citizens' thirst for booze wasn't eliminated by government mandate, and gangs made fortunes dealing in illegal beer, gin and other intoxicants. Capone reveled in the hypocrisy of a society that banned booze and then paid him a fortune to sell it. He remained the mob boss from 1924 to 1931, until Eliot Ness brought him down on tax evasion charges. Ness was the federal agent whose task force earned the name 'The Untouchables' because its members were supposedly impervious to bribes. Capone served his jail sentence from 1932 to 1939. By the time he left, he was disabled by syphilis.

Sites to See
Infamous Capone sites to see include **Holy Name Cathedral** (735 N State St, Near North), where Capone ordered a couple of hits that took place near the church. You'll have to use your imagination for the **St Valentine's Day Massacre Site** (2122 N Clark St, Lincoln Park), where Capone's thugs killed seven members of Bugs Moran's gang. The area is now a parking lot. The Green Mill (p87) was the Capone's favorite speakeasy. The gangster is buried in Mt Carmel Cemetery in suburban Hillside. His simple gravestone reads, 'Alphonse Capone, 1899–1947, My Jesus Mercy.'

Explore

Gold Coast

The Gold Coast has been the address of Chicago's wealthiest residents for more than 125 years. Bejeweled women glide in and out of the neighborhood's stylish boutiques. The occasional Rolls Royce wheels along the leafy streets. The 360° Chicago observatory and Museum of Contemporary Art are the top attention grabbers. At night, Rush St entertains with swanky steakhouses and piano lounges.

The Sights in a Day

Breakfast at **Hendrickx Belgian Bread Crafter** (p64) is a sweet affair. Afterward take a stroll on **Oak Street Beach** (p62), then see what head-scratching exhibits are on at the **Museum of Contemporary Art** (p58).

Book lovers should check out the **Newberry Library** (p62), while fans of antique hemorrhoid surgery kits should peruse the **International Museum of Surgical Science** (p62). If you're at the latter, be sure to walk down nearby Astor St and behold the elegant manors, including Hugh Hefner's **Original Playboy Mansion** (p62).

Nighttime is prime time to take the lickety-split elevator up 94 floors to the **360° Chicago** (p56) observatory. Then again, you could go higher – to the 96th floor – and see the same view from the **Signature Lounge** (p64). For dinner, join the chichi crowd at **Gibson's** (p63) or have romantic French-Vietnamese fare at **Le Colonial** (p63).

👁 Top Sights

360° Chicago (p56)

Museum of Contemporary Art (p58)

🖤 Best of Chicago

Drinking & Nightlife
Signature Lounge (p64)

Eating
Hendrickx Belgian Bread Crafter (p64)

For Kids
American Girl Place (p65)

Lego Store (p65)

Museums & Galleries
Museum of Contemporary Art (p58)

International Museum of Surgical Science (p62)

Architecture
360° Chicago (p56)

Water Tower (p62)

Getting There

Ⓜ **El** Red Line to Clark/Division for the neighborhood's northern reaches; Red Line to Chicago for the southern areas.

🚌 **Bus** Number 151 runs along Michigan Ave, handy for further-flung sights.

Top Sights
360° Chicago

In the John Hancock Center, the city's fourth-tallest skyscraper, 360° Chicago is a dandy place to get high. In many ways the view here surpasses the one at Willis Tower, as the Hancock is closer to the lake and provides unfettered panoramic vistas. If that's not enough, the observatory offers a couple of lofty thrill features as well.

👁 Map p60, C7

www.360chicago.com

875 N Michigan Ave, John Hancock Center, 94th fl

adult/child $20.50/13.50

🕙9am-11pm

Ⓜ Red Line to Chicago

Observatory Lowdown

The 94th-floor observatory offers informative displays that tell you the names of the surrounding buildings. It has the Skywalk, a sort of screened-in porch that lets you feel the wind and hear the city sounds. The biggest draw is TILT, floor-to-ceiling windows that you stand in as they move and tip out over the ground; it costs $7 extra and is actually less spine-tingling than it sounds. The observatory is probably your best bet if you have kids or if you're a newbie and want to beef up your Chicago knowledge, but there are other options.

Observatory Alternatives

Not interested in frivolities? Shoot straight up to the 96th-floor Signature Lounge (p64), where the view is free if you buy a drink ($8 to $16). That's right, here you'll get a glass of wine and a comfy seat while staring out at almost identical views from a few floors higher than the observatory. The elevators for the lounge (and its companion restaurant on the 95th floor) are separate from those for the observatory. Look for signs that say 'Signature 95th/96th' one floor up from the observatory entrance.

Architecture

The Hancock Center was completed in 1969. Fazlur Khan and Bruce Graham were the chief architects, and they designed the structure to sway 5in to 8in in Chicago's windy conditions. They went on to build the Willis Tower four years later.

☑ Top Tips

▶ Go at night, when the views are particularly awesome. On Wednesday and Saturday evenings in summer there's the bonus of seeing Navy Pier's fireworks.

▶ Feel the speed as you ascend in the elevators. They're moving at 20mph.

▶ If you're short on time, the Hancock observatory is often less crowded than the one at Willis Tower.

✗ Take a Break

Join dapper residents from the neighboring high-rises for a Manhattan at the Coq d'Or (p64) lounge. Hendrickx Belgian Bread Crafter (p64) hits the spot for waffles and other sweet treats.

Top Sights
Museum of Contemporary Art

Consider it the Art Institute's brash, rebellious sibling, with especially strong minimalist, surrealist and conceptual photography collections. Covering art from the 1920s onward, the MCA's displays are arranged to blur the boundaries between painting, sculpture, video and other media. Exhibits change regularly so you never know what you'll see, but count on it being offbeat and provocative.

◉ Map p60, D8

www.mcachicago.org

220 E Chicago Ave

adult/child $15/free

⊙10am-8pm Tue, to 5pm Wed-Sun

Ⓜ Red Line to Chicago

Exhibitions

The Museum of Contemporary Art mounts themed exhibitions that typically focus on underappreciated or up-and-coming artists that curators are introducing to American audiences. For example, you might see the first solo show in the US of Nigerian artist Otobong Nkanga's tapestries, or Turner Prize winner Simon Starling's mixed-media works made of recycled materials. Shows last three months or so before the galleries morph into something new.

Sculpture Garden & Front Plaza

The terraced sculpture garden at the back of the museum makes for a nifty browse. In summer a jazz band plays amid the greenery every Tuesday at 5:30pm. Patrons bring blankets and sip drinks from the bar. The museum's front plaza also sees lots of action, especially on Tuesday mornings when a farmers market with veggies, cheeses and baked goods sets up from 7am to 2pm June to October. Both events are big local to-dos.

Arty Theater

The Museum of Contemporary Art's theater regularly hosts dance, music and film events by contemporary A-listers. Much of it is pretty far out, eg an Inuit throat singer performing to a silent-film backdrop, a play about ventriloquists performed by a European puppet troupe, or nude male dancers leaping in a piece about how technology affects life. Bonus: a theater ticket stub provides free museum admission any time during the week after the show.

☑ **Top Tips**

▶ Docents lead free, 45-minute tours through the galleries daily at 1pm, as well as Tuesdays at 2pm, and weekends at 2pm, and 3pm. Meet at the 2nd-floor visitor service desk.

▶ Tuesdays are often crowded, as locals can visit for free on that day.

▶ The museum's shop wins big points for its groovy books, gifts and children's toys.

✗ **Take a Break**

Marisol, the MCA's stylish restaurant, serves locally sourced small plates, wines and aperitifs. It stays open beyond museum hours. The city's most viewtastic bar is a few blocks away at the Signature Lounge (p64), 96 floors up in the Hancock Center.

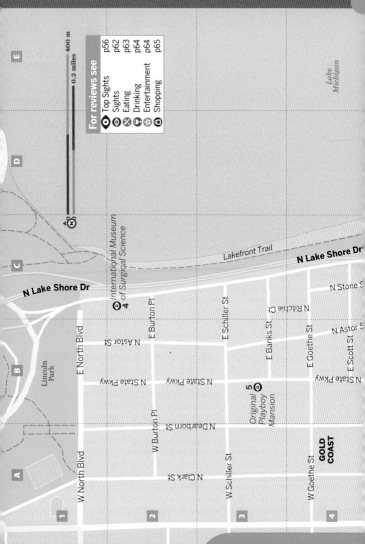

400 m
0.2 miles

For reviews see

◉	Top Sights	p56
◉	Sights	p62
❊	Eating	p63
●	Drinking	p64
❂	Entertainment	p64
⑪	Shopping	p65

Lake Michigan

Lakefront Trail

N Lake Shore Dr

N Lake Shore Dr

International Museum of Surgical Science
◉ 4

N Stone S

N Ritchie Ct

E Schiller St

E Burton Pl

N Astor St

E Banks St

N Astor S

E Goethe St

E Scott St

Lincoln Park

E North Blvd

N State Pkwy

N State Pkwy

N State Pkwy

N State Pkwy

Original Playboy Mansion
◉ 5

W North Blvd

W Burton Pl

N Dearborn St

GOLD COAST

W Goethe St

N Clark St

W Schiller St

W Goethe St

NEAR NORTH

N Lake Shore Dr

N Lake Shore Dr

Northwestern University Chicago Campus

Oak Street Beach **3** ⊙

E Lake Shore Dr

N Dewitt Pl

E Walton St

Lake Shore Park

Museum of Contemporary Art ⊙

E Pearson St

N Mies van der Rohe Way

Water Tower Place

Seneca Park

E Chicago Ave

John Hancock Center **9** ⊙

360° Chicago

14 Ⓜ **15**

13 ✿

10 Ⓜ

E Elm St

E Cedar St

E Bellevue Pl

E Oak St

E Walton St

N Michigan Ave

E Chestnut St

Water Tower **2** ⊙

N Rush St

N Wabash Ave

N Rush St **6** ✕

7 ✕

N State St

E Delaware Pl

8 ✕

Ⓜ Chicago

11 Ⓜ

W Elm St

W Maple St

N Dearborn St

12 ✿

W Oak St

N Clark St

Newberry Library **1** ⊙

E Delaware Pl

W Chestnut St

W Delaware Pl

W Chicago Ave

Clark/Division

Sights

Newberry Library
LIBRARY

1 🎯 Map p60, A7

The Newberry's public galleries are for bibliophiles: those who swoon over original Thomas Paine pamphlets about the French Revolution, or get weak-kneed seeing Thomas Jefferson's copy of the *History of the Expedition under Captains Lewis and Clark* (with margin notes!). Intriguing exhibits rotate yellowed manuscripts and tattered first editions from the library's extensive collection. The on site bookstore is tops for Chicago-themed tomes. (📞312-943-9090; www.newberry.org; 60 W Walton St; admission free; 🕙galleries 8:15am-5pm Mon, Fri & Sat, to 7:30pm Tue-Thu; Ⓜ Red Line to Chicago)

Water Tower
LANDMARK

2 🎯 Map p60, C8

The 154ft-tall, turreted tower is a defining city icon: it was the sole downtown survivor of the 1871 Great Chicago Fire, thanks to its yellow limestone bricks, which withstood the flames. Today the tower houses the free **City Gallery** (📞312-742-0808; admission free; 🕙10am-6:30pm), showcasing Chicago-themed works by local photographers and artists and is well worth a peek. (108 N Michigan Ave; Ⓜ Red Line to Chicago)

Oak Street Beach
BEACH

3 🎯 Map p60, D5

This beach packs in bodies beautiful at the edge of downtown in the shadow of skyscrapers. Lifeguards are on duty in summer. You can rent umbrellas and lounge chairs. The island-y, yellow-umbrella-dotted cafe provides drinks and DJs. (www.cpdbeaches.com; 1000 N Lake Shore Dr; Ⓜ Red Line to Chicago)

International Museum of Surgical Science
MUSEUM

4 🎯 Map p60, C2

Amputation saws, iron lungs and other early tools of the trade are strewn throughout this creaky mansion. The ancient Roman vaginal speculum leaves a lasting impression, while the pointy-ended hemorrhoid surgery instruments serve as a reminder to eat lots of fiber. The collection of 'stones' (as in 'kidney-' and 'gall-') and bloodletting displays look equally painful. (📞312-642-6502; www.imss.org; 1524 N Lake Shore Dr; adult/child $15/7; 🕙10am-4pm Tue-Fri, to 5pm Sat & Sun; 🚌151)

Original Playboy Mansion
NOTABLE BUILDING

5 🎯 Map p60, B3

The sexual revolution started in the basement 'grotto' of this 1899 manor. Hugh Hefner bought the mansion in 1959 and hung a brass plate over the door warning 'If You Don't Swing, Don't Ring.' Heavy partying ensued. In the mid-1970s, Hef decamped to LA. The building contains condos now, but a visit still allows you to boast 'I've been to the Playboy Mansion.' (1340 N State Pkwy; Ⓜ Red Line to Clark/Division)

Original Playboy Mansion

Eating

Le Colonial FRENCH, VIETNAMESE $$$

6 🍴 Map p60, B6

Step into the dark-wood, candle-lit room, where ceiling fans swirl lazily and big-leafed palms sway in the breeze, and you'd swear you were in 1920s Saigon. Staff can arrange vegetarian and gluten-free substitutions among the curries and banana-leaf-wrapped fish dishes. If you want spicy, be specific; everything typically comes out mild. (📞312-255-0088; www.lecolonial chicago.com; 937 N Rush St; mains $22-32; ⏰11:30am-3pm & 5-10pm Sun-Thu, to 11pm Fri & Sat; 🖊; Ⓜ Red Line to Chicago)

Gibson's STEAK $$$

7 🍴 Map p60, B6

Politicians, movers, shakers and the shaken-down swirl martinis and compete for prime table space in the dining room of this local original. The rich and beautiful mingle at the bar. As for the meat on the plates, the steaks and lobsters are as good as they come. (📞312-266-8999; www.gibsonssteakhouse. com; 1028 N Rush St; mains $45-60; ⏰11am-midnight; Ⓜ Red Line to Clark/Division)

Tempo Cafe AMERICAN $

8 🍴 Map p60, B7

Bright and cheery, this diner brings most of its meals to the table the way

Local Life

Hendrickx Belgian Bread Crafter

Hiding in a nondescript apartment building, **Hendrickx Belgian Bread Crafter** (Map p61, C6; ☎312-649-6717; www.hendrickxbakery.com; 100 E Walton St; mains $5-12.50; ⊙8am-3:30pm Mon, to 7pm Tue-Sat, 9am-3pm Sun; Ⓜ Red Line to Chicago) is a local secret. Open the bright orange door and behold the waffles, white-chocolate bread and dark-chocolate croissants among the flaky, buttery, Belgian treats. The place is tiny, with just a few indoor seats, but in warm weather it sets up tables on the sidewalk.

they're meant to be served – in a skillet. The omelet-centric menu includes all manner of fresh veggies and meat, as well as sandwiches. It's nothing fancy, but it's open round the clock and makes for a relatively cheap meal in the pricey Gold Coast. (☎312-943-4373; www.tempochicago.com; 6 E Chestnut St; mains $9-15; ⊙24hr; Ⓜ Red Line to Chicago)

Drinking

Signature Lounge
LOUNGE

9 Map p60, C7

Take the elevator to the 96th floor of the John Hancock Center and order a drink while viewing the city from some 1000ft up in the sky. It's particularly gape-worthy at night. Ladies: don't miss the bathroom view. (www.signature room.com; 875 N Michigan Ave, John Hancock

Center, 96th fl; ⊙11am-12:30am Sun-Thu, to 1:30am Fri & Sat; Ⓜ Red Line to Chicago)

Coq d'Or
LOUNGE

10 Map p60, C6

This classy joint in the Drake Hotel opened the day after Prohibition was repealed. It offers a taste of old Chicago: burgundy-colored leather booths, snazzy bartenders and bejeweled women in furs sipping Manhattans. A pianist starts tinkling the ivories around 9pm on weekends. (☎312-932-4623; 140 E Walton St; ⊙11am-1am Sun-Thu, to 2am Fri & Sat; Ⓜ Red Line to Chicago)

Sparrow
COCKTAIL BAR

11 Map p60, B5

This refined lounge, inspired by hotel lobby bars of the 1930 and '40s, is a hidden gem in Chicago's Gold Coast. Tucked behind a modest storefront in an art-deco apartment building, Sparrow emphasizes rum-focused cocktails, but there's also an extensive wine list and 10 rotating beers on tap. It's a great place to duck into after a dinner downtown. (☎312-725-0732; www.sparrowchicago. com; 12 W Elm St; ⊙4pm-2am Sun-Fri, to 3am Sat; Ⓜ Red Line to Clark/Division)

Entertainment

Chicago Children's Theatre
THEATER

12 Map p60, A6

CCT is dedicated exclusively to putting on quality productions for young audiences. Many plays are adapted from children's books, and many use puppets or music. The group is building a swanky new theater in the West Loop to be completed in 2020. Until then, performances take place at the Ruth Page Center for Arts. (CCT; ☏773-227-0180; www.chicagochildrenstheatre.org; 1016 N Dearborn St; Ⓜ Red Line to Clark/Division)

Lookingglass Theatre Company
THEATER

13 ⭐ Map p60, C8

This well-regarded troupe works in a nifty theater hewn from the old **Water Works** (163 E Pearson St; ⊘9am-7pm Mon-Thu, 9am-6pm Fri & Sat, 11am-5pm Sun) building. The ensemble cast – which includes co-founder David Schwimmer of TV's *Friends* – often uses physical stunts and acrobatics to enhance its dreamy, magical, literary productions. (☏312-337-0665; www.lookingglasstheatre.org; 821 N Michigan Ave; Ⓜ Red Line to Chicago)

Shopping
American Girl Place
TOYS

14 🔒 Map p60, C7

This doll shop is a fun experience! Dolls are treated as humans: the 'hospital' uses wheelchairs for repairs, and the cafe seats the dolls as part of the family during tea service. While there are American Girl stores in many cities, this flagship remains the largest and busiest. (☏877-247-5223; www.americangirl.com; 835 N Michigan Ave, Water Tower Place; ⊘10am-8pm Mon-Thu, to 9pm Fri, 9am-9pm Sat, 9am-6pm Sun; ♿; Ⓜ Red Line to Chicago)

Lego Store
TOYS

15 🔒 Map p60, C8

After marvelling at the cool models of rockets, castles and dinosaurs scattered throughout the store, kids can build their own designs at pint-sized tables equipped with bins of the signature little bricks. (www.lego.com; 835 N Michigan Ave, 2nd fl; ⊘10am-9pm Mon-Sat, 11am-6pm Sun; ♿; Ⓜ Red Line to Chicago)

Understand
Astor Street

In the 1880s Chicago's rich and powerful families began moving to Astor St and trying to outdo each other with palatial homes. The mansions rising up in the 1300 to 1500 blocks reflect the grandeur of that heady period. **Cyrus McCormick Mansion** (1500 N Astor St; 🚇151) is a neighborhood standout. New York architect Stanford White designed the 1893 neoclassical beauty, which is now divided into luxury condos. The 1885 **Archbishop's Residence** (1555 N State Pkwy;) is another eye-popper, complete with 19 chimneys. Alas, the current archbishop does not live on site, though the diocese still owns the building.

Explore

Lincoln Park
& Old Town

Lincoln Park – the green space – is the city's premier playground of lagoons, footpaths, beaches and zoo animals. Lincoln Park – the surrounding neighborhood – adds top-notch restaurants, kicky shops, and lively blues and rock clubs to the mix. Next door, stylish Old Town hangs on to its free-spirited past with artsy bars and improv-comedy bastion Second City.

The Sights in a Day

Begin with a wander in **Lincoln Park** (p68). You could spend the whole morning communing with lions, zebras and polar bears at **Lincoln Park Zoo** (p72). For a more tranquil scene, browse the blooms at **Lincoln Park Conservatory** (p73) or meet the butterflies at **Peggy Notebaert Nature Museum** (p73).

Head south for fun in the sun at North Avenue Beach (pictured left). **Chicago History Museum** (p72) is nearby, where you can see the bell worn by Mrs O'Leary's cow (the bovine that took the rap for starting the 1871 Great Fire). Head into Old Town on Wells St, filled with browsable spots such as **Spice House** (p77) and **La Fournette** (p74).

If multiple courses of molecular gastronomy sounds good, try to score seats at **Alinea** (p74). If not, make it an evening of improv at **Second City** (p76), followed by drinks at the **Old Town Ale House** (p75). Then again, you could do pizza at **Pequod's** (p74) and blues at **Kingston Mines** (p77) or **BLUES** (p77).

Top Sight

Lincoln Park (p68)

Best of Chicago

Comedy & Performing Arts
Second City (p76)

iO Theater (p76)

Steppenwolf Theatre (p76)

Eating
Alinea (p74)

Pequod's Pizza (p74)

Wieners Circle (p75)

Drinking & Nightlife
Old Town Ale House (p75)

Delilah's (p76)

Live Music
BLUES (p77)

Lincoln Hall (p77)

Kingston Mines (p77)

Sports & Activities
North Avenue Beach (p72)

Getting There

El Brown, Purple, Red Line to Fullerton for Lincoln Park; Brown, Purple Line to Sedgwick for Old Town.

Bus 151 from downtown (Michigan Ave) for the zoo and parks.

Top Sights
Lincoln Park

The neighborhood gets its name from this park, Chicago's largest. Its 1200 acres stretch for 6 miles from North Ave north to Diversey Pkwy, where it narrows and continues until the end of Lake Shore Dr. On sunny days locals come out to play in droves, taking advantage of the ponds, paths and playing fields or visiting the zoo and beaches.

👁 Map p70, G4

🕐 6am-11pm

🚌 151

Lincoln Park Conservatory (p73)

Zoo & Other Freebies

Opened in 1868, the free Lincoln Park Zoo (p72) has entertained generations of Chicagoans. Families swarm the grounds, which are smack in the park's midst. Kids beeline for the Regenstein African exhibit, which puts them close to pygmy hippos and dwarf crocodiles. The Ape House pleases with its swingin' gorillas and chimps. Snow monkeys chill in the Macaque Forest. The leafy conservatory (p73) and hidden **lily garden** (www.lincolnparkconservancy.org; 2391 N Stockton Dr; admission free; ⏰7:30am-dusk mid-Apr–mid-Nov; 🚌151) are also nearby and free.

Lincoln & the Mausoleum

At the park's southern edge, sculptor Augustus Saint-Gaudens' **Standing Lincoln** (🚌22) shows the 16th president deep in contemplation before giving a speech. Saint-Gaudens based the work on casts made of Lincoln's face and hands while Lincoln was alive. The statue stands behind the Chicago History Museum (p72).

Nearby, at the corner of LaSalle Dr and Clark St, take a gander at the **Couch Mausoleum** (🚌22). It's the sole reminder of the land's pre-1864 use, when it was a municipal cemetery. Many graves contained dead soldiers from Camp Douglas, a horrific prisoner-of-war stockade on the city's South Side during the Civil War. The city eventually relocated the bodies.

Beaches & Beyond

There's more beyond the zoo, gardens and monuments. Head north and there are sailboat harbors, golf courses, bird sanctuaries and rowing clubs gliding on the lagoons. Walk east from anywhere in the park and you'll come to the Lakefront Trail that connects several beaches along the way.

☑ Top Tips

▶ Markets and takeaway joints pop up along Clark St and Diversey Pkwy, prime for picnic provisions.

▶ Convenient Divvy stations to grab a bike for a short ride are at the corner of Lake Shore Dr and North Blvd, and at the Theater on the Lake building (near the intersection of Lake Shore Dr and W Fullerton Pkwy).

▶ Visit the park on Wednesday or Saturday morning to experience Green City Market's bounty as a bonus to your jaunt.

✗ Take a Break

Sultan's Market (p75) does the trick for a casual Middle Eastern meal. The J Parker (p76) provides a swanky break at its rooftop cocktail bar.

A | B | C | D

1

W Wrightwood Ave

14

N Lincoln Ave

N Surrey Ct

N Racine Ave

N Seminary Ave

W Wrightwood Ave

W Lill Ave
21

19
W Altgeld St

N Halsted St

N Burling St

N Orchard St

W Deming Pl

N Clark

W Arlington Pl

W Montana St
20

Fullerton

W Fullerton Ave

2

N Wayne Ave

N Lakewood Ave

DePaul University

DePaul Art Museum
7

LINCOLN PARK

W Belden Ave

W Belden Ave

N Geneva Tce

N Lincoln Ave

W Webster Ave

3

9

N Magnolia Ave

N Racine Ave

N Clifton Ave

N Seminary Ave

N Kenmore Ave

N Sheffield Ave

N Bissell St

N Fremont St

N Dayton St

N Halsted St

Oz Park

N Larrabee St

W Dickens Ave

W Armitage Ave

Armitage

W Cortland St

4

North Branch Chicago River

N Maud Ave

N Clybourn Ave

N Marcey St

N Bissell St

W Wisconsin St

N Burling St

N Orchard St

N Howe St

N Larrabee St

N Mohawk St

N Kingsbury St

N Willow St

W Willow St

W Willow St

OLD TOWN

N Dayton St

8

18

5

W North Ave

North/Clybourn

17

N 0 ___ 500 m
0 ___ 0.25 miles

E

N Lakeview Ave
N Cannon Dr
Diversey Harbor

North Pond

N Stockton Dr

Lincoln Park

Peggy Notebaert Nature Museum 6 ✩

N Lake Shore Dr

Fullerton Beach ✘

W Fullerton Pkwy

5 ◎ Lincoln Park Conservatory

N Clark St

N Lincoln Park W

W Webster Ave

Lincoln Park Zoo ◎ 4

Lake Michigan

P

W Dickens Ave

Lincoln Park Zoo

N Cannon Dr

South Lagoon

N Lincoln Ave

N Stockton Dr

N Hudson Ave

W Wisconsin St

South Pond

Lincoln Park

W Menomonee St 15 ✘◎ 3
W Willow St

Green City Market

N Clark St
N Wells St

North Avenue Beach

Lincoln Park ⊙

N Lake Shore Dr

N Hudson Ave
N Sedgwick St

W Eugenie St
✘ 11

W LaSalle Dr

2 ◎ North Avenue Beach

16 ✩

Chicago History Museum

1 ◎

W North Ave

Ⓜ Sedgwick

🍷 13 ✘ 10

N LaSalle Dr

E North Blvd

N Astor St

🛍 22

Sights

Chicago History Museum

MUSEUM

1 ◎ Map p70, F5

Curious about Chicago's storied past? Multimedia displays at this museum cover it all, from the Great Fire to the 1968 Democratic Convention. President Lincoln's deathbed is here, as is the bell worn by Mrs O'Leary's cow. So is the chance to 'become' a Chicago hot dog covered in condiments (in the kids' area, but adults are welcome for the photo op). (✆312-642-4600; www.chicagohistory. org; 1601 N Clark St; adult/child $16/free; ⏱9:30am-4:30pm Mon & Wed-Sat, to 7:30pm Tue, noon-5pm Sun; ♿; ☐22)

North Avenue Beach

BEACH

2 ◎ Map p70, H4

Chicago's most popular strand of sand wafts a southern California vibe. Buff teams spike volleyballs, kids build sandcastles and everyone jumps in for a swim when the weather heats up. Bands and DJs rock the steamboat-shaped beach house, which serves ice cream and margaritas in equal measure. Kayaks, jet-skis, stand-up paddleboards, bicycles and lounge chairs are available to rent, and there are daily beach yoga classes. (www.cpdbeaches.com; 1600 N Lake Shore Dr; ♿; ☐151)

Green City Market

MARKET

3 ◎ Map p70, F4

Stands of purple cabbages, red radishes, green asparagus and other bright-hued produce sprawl through Lincoln Park at Chicago's biggest farmers market. Follow your nose to the demonstration tent, where local cooks such as *Top Chef* winner Stephanie Izard prepare dishes – say rice crepes with a mushroom *gastrique* – using market ingredients. (✆773-880-1266; www.greencitymarket. org; 1790 N Clark St; ⏱7am-1pm Wed & Sat May-Oct; ☐22)

Lincoln Park Zoo

ZOO

4 ◎ Map p70, F3

The zoo has been around since 1868 and is a local freebie favorite, filled with lions, zebras, snow monkeys and other exotic creatures in the shadow of downtown. Check out the Regenstein African Journey, polar-bear-stocked Arctic Tundra and dragonfly-dappled Nature Boardwalk for the cream of the crop. The Gateway Pavilion (on Cannon Dr) is the main entrance; pick up a map and schedule of feedings and training sessions. (✆312-742-2000; www. lpzoo.org; 2200 N Cannon Dr; admission free; ⏱10am-5pm Mon-Fri, to 6:30pm Sat & Sun Jun-Aug, 10am-5pm Apr, May, Sep & Oct, 10am-4:30pm Nov-Mar; ♿; ☐151)

Polar bear close up, Lincoln Park Zoo

Lincoln Park Conservatory
GARDENS

5 🎯 Map p70, F2

Walking through the Lincoln Park Conservatory's three acres of desert palms, jungle ferns and tropical orchids is like taking a trip around the world in 30 minutes. The glass-bedecked hothouse remains a sultry 75°F escape even in winter. (📞312-742-7736; www.lincolnparkconservancy. org; 2391 N Stockton Dr; admission free; ⏰9am-5pm; 🚌151)

Peggy Notebaert Nature Museum
MUSEUM

6 🎯 Map p70, F2

This hands-on museum has turtles and croaking frogs in its 1st-floor marsh, fluttering insects in its 2nd-floor butterfly haven and a bird boardwalk meandering through its rooftop garden. It's geared mostly to kids. Check the schedule for daily creature feedings. In winter, the Green City Market (p72) sets up inside on Saturday. (📞773-755-5100; www.naturemuseum.org; 2430 N Cannon Dr; adult/child $9/6; ⏰9am-5pm Mon-Fri, 10am-5pm Sat & Sun; 🚼; 🚌151)

Top Tip

Sightseeing from the El

The El (short for 'elevated') train provides a great cheap sightseeing tour of the city. For the best views, hop on the Brown Line and ride into the Loop. Get on in Lincoln Park at either the Fullerton or Armitage stops, take a seat by the window and watch as the train clatters downtown, swinging past skyscrapers so close you can almost touch them.

DePaul Art Museum   MUSEUM

7 Map p70, B2

DePaul University's compact art museum hosts changing exhibits of 20th-century works. Pieces from the permanent collection – by sculptor Claes Oldenburg, cartoonist Chris Ware, architect Daniel Burnham and more – hang on the 2nd floor. It's definitely worth swinging through if you're in the neighborhood; you can see everything in less than 30 minutes. (☏773-325-7506; http://museums.depaul.edu; 935 W Fullerton Ave; admission free; ⏰11am-7pm Wed & Thu, to 5pm Fri, noon-5pm Sat & Sun; Ⓜ Brown, Purple, Red Line to Fullerton)

Eating

Alinea   GASTRONOMY $$$

8 Map p70, C5

One of the world's best restaurants, with three Michelin stars, Alinea brings on multiple courses of molecular gastronomy. Dishes may emanate from a centrifuge or be pressed into a capsule, à la duck served with a 'pillow of lavender air.' There are no reservations; instead Alinea sells tickets two to three months in advance via its website. Check Twitter (@Alinea) for last-minute seats. (☏312-867-0110; www.alinearestaurant.com; 1723 N Halsted St; 10-/16-course menu from $165/285; ⏰5-10pm Wed-Sun; Ⓜ Red Line to North/Clybourn)

Pequod's Pizza   PIZZA $

9 Map p70, A3

Like the ship in *Moby Dick,* from which this neighborhood restaurant takes its name, Pequod's pan-style (akin to deep dish) pizza is a thing of legend – head and shoulders above chain competitors because of its caramelized cheese, generous toppings and sweetly flavored sauce. Neon beer signs glow from the walls, and Blackhawks jerseys hang from the ceiling in the affably rugged interior. (☏773-327-1512; www.pequodspizza.com; 2207 N Clybourn Ave; small pizzas from $12; ⏰11am-2am Mon-Sat, to midnight Sun; 🚌9 to Webster)

La Fournette   BAKERY $

10 Map p70, F5

The chef hails from Alsace in France and he fills his narrow, rustic-wood bakery with bright-hued macarons (purple passionfruit, green pistachio, red raspberry-chocolate), cheese-infused breads, crust-crackling baguettes and buttery croissants. They all beg to be devoured on the spot with a cup of locally roasted Intelligentsia coffee. Staff make delicious soups, crepes, quiches and sandwiches with equal French love. (312-624-9430; www.lafournette.com; 1547 N Wells St; items $3-7; 7am-6:30pm Mon-Sat, to 5:30pm Sun; Brown, Purple Line to Sedgwick)

Twin Anchors BARBECUE $$

11 Map p70, E5

Twin Anchors is synonymous with ribs – smoky, tangy-sauced baby backs in this case. The meat drops from the ribs as soon as you lift them. The restaurant doesn't take reservations, so you'll have to wait outside or around the neon-lit 1950s bar, which sets the tone for the place. An almost-all-Sinatra jukebox completes the supperclub ambience. (312-266-1616; www.twinanchorsribs.com; 1655 N Sedgwick St; mains $17-28; 5-10:30pm Mon-Thu, to midnight Fri, noon-midnight Sat, noon-10:30pm Sun; Brown, Purple Line to Sedgwick)

Wieners Circle AMERICAN $

12 Map p70, D1

As famous for its unruly, foul-mouthed ambience as its charred hot dogs and cheddar fries, the Wieners Circle is a scene for late-night munchies. During the day and on weeknights it's a normal hot-dog stand – with damn good food. The wild show is on weekend eves, around 2am, when the nearby bars close and

everyone starts yelling. The f-bombs fly and it can get raucous between staff and customers. (773-477-7444; 2622 N Clark St; hot dogs $3-7; 11am-4am Sun-Thu, to 5am Fri & Sat; Brown, Purple Line to Diversey)

Drinking

Old Town Ale House BAR

13 Map p70, F5

Located near the Second City comedy club and the scene of late-night musings since the 1960s, this unpretentious neighborhood favorite lets you mingle with beautiful people and grizzled regulars, seated pint by pint under the nude-politician paintings. Classic jazz on the jukebox provides the soundtrack for the jovial goings-on. Cash only. (312-944-7020; www.theoldtownalehouse.com; 219 W North Ave; 3pm-4am Mon-Fri, from noon Sat & Sun; Brown, Purple Line to Sedgwick)

Local Life
Sultan's Market

Neighborhood folks dig the falafel sandwiches, spinach pies and other quality Middle Eastern fare at family run **Sultan's Market** (Map p70,D1; 872-253-1489; 2521 N Clark St; mains $4-7; 10am-10pm Mon-Sat, to 9pm Sun; Brown, Purple, Red Line to Fullerton). The small, homey space doesn't have many tables, but Lincoln Park is nearby for picnicking.

Delilah's
BAR

14 Map p70, B1

A bartender rightfully referred to this hard-edged black sheep of the neighborhood as the 'pride of Lincoln Ave' – a title earned for the heavy pours and the best whiskey selection in the city. The no-nonsense staff know their way around a beer list, too, tapping unusual domestic and international suds. Cheap Pabst longnecks are always behind the bar as well. (773-472-2771; www.delilahschicago.com; 2771 N Lincoln Ave; 4pm-2am Sun-Fri, to 3am Sat; Brown Line to Diversey)

J Parker
LOUNGE

15 Map p70, F4

It's all about the view from the Hotel Lincoln's 13th-floor rooftop bar. And it delivers, sweeping over the park, the lake and downtown skyline. Prepare to jostle with the young and preppy crowd, especially if it's a warm night. (312-254-4747; www.jparkerchicago.com; 1816 N Clark St, 13th fl; 5pm-1am Mon-Thu, from 3pm Fri, from 11:30am Sat & Sun; 22)

Entertainment

Second City
COMEDY

16 Map p70, F5

Bill Murray, Stephen Colbert, Tina Fey and more honed their wit at this slick venue where shows take place nightly. The Mainstage and ETC stage host sketch revues (with an improv scene thrown in); they're similar in price and quality. If you turn up around 10pm (on any night except Friday and Saturday) you can have yourself a bargain and watch the comics improv a set for free. (312-337-3992; www.secondcity.com; 1616 N Wells St; tickets $29-36; Brown, Purple Line to Sedgwick)

iO Theater
COMEDY

17 Map p70, B5

One of Chicago's top-tier improv houses, iO is a bit edgier (and cheaper) than its competition, with four stages hosting bawdy shows nightly. Two bars and a beer garden add to the fun. The Improvised Shakespeare Company is awesome; catch them if you can. (312-929-2401; www.ioimprov.com/chicago; 1501 N Kingsbury St; tickets $5-16; Red Line to North/Clybourn)

Steppenwolf Theatre
THEATER

18 Map p70, C5

Steppenwolf is Chicago's top stage for quality, provocative theater productions. The Hollywood-heavy ensemble includes Gary Sinise, John Malkovich, Martha Plimpton, Gary Cole, Joan Allen and Tracy Letts. A money-saving tip: the box office releases 20 tickets for $20 for each day's shows; they go on sale at 11am Monday to Saturday and at 1pm Sunday, and are available by phone. (312-335-1650; www.steppenwolf.org; 1650 N Halsted St; Red Line to North/Clybourn)

BLUES

BLUES

19 ⭐ Map p70, C1

Long, narrow and high volume, this veteran blues club draws a slightly older crowd that soaks up every crackling, electrified moment. As one local musician put it, 'The audience here comes out to *understand* the blues.' Big local names grace the small stage. (☏773-528-1012; www.chicagobluesbar. com; 2519 N Halsted St; cover charge $7-10; ☻8pm-2am Wed-Sun; Ⓜ Brown, Purple, Red Line to Fullerton)

Lincoln Hall

LIVE MUSIC

20 ⭐ Map p70, C2

Hyped national indie bands are the main players at this ubercool, mid-sized venue with excellent sound. The front room has a kitchen that offers small plates and sandwiches until 10pm. (☏773-525-2501; www.lh-st.com; 2424 N Lincoln Ave; 🛜; Ⓜ Brown, Purple, Red Line to Fullerton)

Kingston Mines

BLUES

21 ⭐ Map p70, C1

Popular enough to draw big names on the blues circuit, Kingston Mines is so noisy, hot and sweaty that blues neophytes will feel as though they're having a genuine experience – sort of like a gritty Delta theme park. Two stages, seven nights a week, ensure somebody's always on. The blues jam session from 6pm to 8pm on Sunday is free. (☏773-477-4646; www.kingston mines.com; 2548 N Halsted St; cover charge $12-15; ☻7:30pm-4am Mon-Thu, 7pm-4am Fri, 7am-5am Sat, 6pm-4am Sun; Ⓜ Brown, Purple, Red Line to Fullerton)

Shopping

Spice House

FOOD

22 🔒 Map p70, F5

A bombardment of fragrance socks you in the nose at this exotic spice house in Old Town, offering delicacies such as black and red volcanic salt from Hawaii and pomegranate molasses among the tidy jars. Best, though, are the housemade herb blends themed after Chicago neighborhoods, such as the Bronzeville Rib Rub, allowing you to take home a taste of the city. (☏312-274-0378; www.thespicehouse. com; 1512 N Wells St; ☻10am-7pm Mon-Sat, to 5pm Sun; Ⓜ Brown, Purple Line to Sedgwick)

Dave's Records

MUSIC

23 🔒 Map p70, D1

Rolling Stone magazine picked Dave's as one of the nation's best record stores. It has an 'all vinyl, all the time' mantra, meaning crate diggers will be in their element flipping through the stacks of rock, jazz, blues, folk and house. Dave himself usually mans the counter, where you'll find a slew of 25-cent cheapie records for sale. (☏773-929-6325; www.davesrecordschicago. com; 2604 N Clark St; ☻11am-8pm Mon-Sat, noon-7pm Sun; Ⓜ Brown, Purple Line to Diversey)

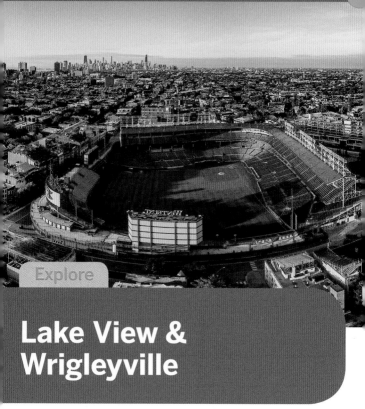

Explore

Lake View & Wrigleyville

The young and frolicsome claim Lake View, reveling in its nonstop lineup of bars, theaters and rock halls. Hallowed Wrigley Field draws baseball pilgrims; and the boozy quarter around it – aka Wrigleyville – parties hard and collides with the rainbow banners of Boystown, Chicago's main gay district, chockablock with dance clubs. Global eateries cater to the masses.

The Sights in a Day

☀ The neighborhood snoozes in the morning. By 11am places start to open so you can wander Halsted St in **Boystown** (p83), where shops sell naughty knickers and gay novelties, or browse Clark St for fun shops like **Strange Cargo** (p85). Fuel up with an early lunch at **Crisp** (p84).

☼ In good weather, nothing beats an afternoon at **Wrigley Field** (p80). The neighborhood jumps with high-fiving sports fans spilling out of bars. Even if there's not a game on, explore the historic ballpark on a tour.

☾ Have dinner at **Home Bistro** (p83) or **mfk** (p83), then get ready to party. Mellower types can drink at **GMan Tavern** (p83). Rock fans should check the schedule at **Metro** (p85), while improv fans should see what's on at **Annoyance Theatre** (p85). Late at night head to **Berlin** (p84) or **Smart Bar** (p84) to shake your tail.

◉ Top Sight

Wrigley Field (p80)

♥ Best of Chicago

Sports & Activities
Chicago Cubs (p85)

Gay & Lesbian
Sidetrack (p84)

Berlin (p84)

Closet (p84)

Home Bistro (p83)

Live Music
Metro (p85)

Eating
mfk (p83)

Drinking & Nightlife
Smart Bar (p84)

Berlin (p84)

Shopping
Strange Cargo (p85)

Getting There

Ⓜ **El** Red Line to Addison for Wrigleyville and around; Red, Brown, Purple Line to Belmont for much of Boystown.

Top Sights
Wrigley Field

Built in 1914, Wrigley Field – aka the Friendly
Confines – is the second-oldest baseball park
in the major leagues. It's filled with legendary
traditions and curses, including a team that
didn't win a championship for 108 years – the
longest dry spell in US sports history. Then in
2016 the Cubs triumphed in mythic style, adding
yet another chapter to this storied venue.

◉ Map p82, B3

www.cubs.com

1060 W Addison St

Ⓜ Red Line to Addison

Environs

The ballpark provides an old-school slice of Americana, with a hand-turned scoreboard, ivy-covered outfield walls and an iconic neon sign over the front entrance. The field is uniquely situated smack in the middle of a neighborhood, surrounded on all sides by houses, bars and restaurants. The grassy plaza just north of the main entrance – aka The Park – has tables, chairs, a coffee shop and huge video screen. On non-game days it's open to the public; on game days it's a beer garden for ticket holders.

The Curse & Its Reverse

It started with Billy Sianis, owner of the Billy Goat Tavern. The year was 1945 and the Cubs were in the World Series against the Detroit Tigers. When Sianis tried to enter Wrigley Field with his pet goat to see the game, ballpark staff refused, saying the goat stank. Sianis threw up his arms and called down a mighty hex, saying that the Cubs would never win another World Series. Years rolled by, and they didn't. Then in 2016 it happened: the Cubs won the Series in a wild, come-from-behind set of games. The curse was exorcised.

The Traditions

When the middle of the seventh inning arrives, it's time for the seventh inning stretch. You then stand up for the group sing-along of 'Take Me Out to the Ballgame,' typically led by a guest celebrity. Here's another tradition: if you catch a home run slugged by the competition, you're honor-bound to throw it back onto the field.

☑ Top Tips

▶ Buy tickets at the Cubs' website or Wrigley box office. Online ticket broker StubHub (www.stubhub.com) is also reliable.

▶ The Upper Reserved Infield seats are usually pretty cheap. They're high up, but have decent views.

▶ Ninety-minute stadium tours ($25) are available most days April through September. Try going on a non-game day, as you'll see more.

✗ Take a Break

It's a pre-game ritual to beer up at **Murphy's Bleachers** (☎773-281-5356; www.murphysbleachers.com; 3655 N Sheffield Ave; ⊙11am-2am; Ⓜ Red Line to Addison; only steps away from the ballpark. Inside Wrigley Field, bite into a gourmet hot dog at the Hot Doug's food stand at Platform 14 (behind the bleachers, though you need a bleacher ticket to get there).

Sights

Boystown   AREA

1 Map p82, D4

What the Castro is to San Francisco, Boystown is to the Windy City. The mecca of queer Chicago (especially for men), the streets of Boystown are full of rainbow flags and packed with bars, shops and restaurants catering to residents of the gay neighborhood. (btwn Halsted St & Broadway, Belmont Ave & Addison St; M Red Line to Addison)

Eating

Home Bistro   AMERICAN $$

2 Map p82, C4

Home Bistro (aka 'HB') feels as cozy as the nouveau comfort food it serves. Cider-soaked mussels, duck meatball gnocchi, and buttermilk fried chicken hit the tables in the wood-and-tile-lined space. Try to snag a seat by the front window, which entertains with Boystown people-watching. You can bring your own wine or beer, which is a nice money saver. (☎773-661-0299; www.home bistrochicago.com; 3404 N Halsted St; mains $20-25; ☺5:30-10pm Tue-Thu, 5-10:30pm Fri & Sat, 11am-9pm Sun; M Red Line to Addison)

mfk   SPANISH $$

3 Map p82, D5

In mfk's teeny space it feels like you're having a romantic meal in Spain, with the sea lapping just outside the door.

Strange Cargo (p85)

Dig into crunchy prawn heads, garlicky octopus and veal meatballs amid the whitewashed walls and ornate tiles. Sunny cocktails and a wine list dominated by whites and rosés add to the goodness. (☎773-857-2540; www.mfkres taurant.com; 432 W Diversey Pkwy; small plates $10-18; ☺5-10pm Mon & Tue, noon-10pm Wed & Thu, to midnight Fri & Sat, to 10pm Sun; ☒22)

Drinking

GMan Tavern   BAR

4 Map p82, B2

The pool tables, large and eclectic beer selection, and pierced-and-tattooed patrons make the GMan wonderfully

Crisp

Music pours from the stereo while delicious Korean fusions arrive from the kitchen at cheerful **Crisp** (Map p82, D5; ☏773-697-7610; www.crisponline.com; 2940 N Broadway; mains $9-13; ⊙11:30am-9pm; ⓜBrown, Purple Line to Wellington) The 'Bad Boy Buddha' bowl, a variation on *bibimbop* (mixed veg with rice), is one of the best healthy lunches in town. Crisp's fried chicken (especially the 'Seoul Sassy' with its savory soy-ginger sauce) also wows the local crowd.

different from the surrounding Wrigleyville sports bars. Bands and DJs often play on the back-room stage. For years the bar was the Gingerman Tavern; new owners took over and dubbed it GMan, though established patrons still use the original name. It's a splendid spot to pass an evening. (☏773-549-2050; www.gmantavern.com; 3740 N Clark St; ⊙3pm-2am Sun-Fri, to 3am Sat; ⓜRed Line to Addison)

Smart Bar CLUB

Smart Bar (see 9 ✿ Map p82, B2) is an unpretentious favorite for dancing, located in the basement of the Metro (p85) rock club. The DJs are often more renowned than you'd expect the intimate space to accommodate. House and techno dominate the turntables. (☏773-549-4140; www.smartbarchicago.com; 3730 N Clark St; tickets $5-15; ⊙10pm-4am Thu-Sun; ⓜRed Line to Addison)

Berlin CLUB

5 Map p82, C4

Looking for a packed, sweaty dance floor? Berlin caters to a mostly gay crowd midweek, though partiers of all stripes jam the place on weekends. Monitors flicker through the latest video dispatches from cult pop and electronic acts, while DJs take the dance floor on trancey detours. (☏773-348-4975; www.berlinchicago.com; 954 W Belmont Ave; ⊙10pm-4am Sun-Wed, from 5pm Thu-Sat; ⓜRed, Brown, Purple Line to Belmont)

Sidetrack CLUB

6 Map p82, C4

Massive Sidetrack thumps dance music for gay and straight crowds alike. Get ready to belt out your Broadway best at the good-time 'show-tune nights' on Sunday and Monday. If the indoor action gets too much, the huge outdoor courtyard beckons. (☏773-477-9189; www.sidetrackchicago.com; 3349 N Halsted St; ⊙3pm-2am Mon-Fri, from 1pm Sat & Sun; ⓜRed, Brown, Purple Line to Belmont)

Closet GAY & LESBIAN

7 Map p82, D4

One of the few lesbian-centric bars in Chicago, the Closet changes mood and tempo at 2am, when the crowd becomes more mixed (male and female), the music gets louder and things get a little rowdier. Cash only. (☏773-477-8533; www.theclosetchicago.com; 3325 N Broadway; ⊙4pm-4am Mon-Fri, from noon Sat & Sun; ☏; ⓜRed, Brown, Purple Line to Belmont)

Entertainment

Chicago Cubs BASEBALL

8 Map p82, B3

The beloved Cubs play at old-time Wrigley Field. For 108 years they didn't win a championship – the longest losing streak in US sports history – but in 2016 the team broke the curse. Games are always packed. Ticket prices vary, but in general you'll be hard-pressed to get in for under $40. The popular bleacher seats cost around $55 or so. (✆800-843-2827; www.cubs.com; 1060 W Addison St; Ⓜ Red Line to Addison)

Metro LIVE MUSIC

9 Map p82, B2

For more than three decades, the Metro has been synonymous with loud rock. Sonic Youth and the Ramones in the '80s. Nirvana and Jane's Addiction in the '90s. White Stripes and the Killers in the new millennium. Each night prepare to hear noise by three or four bands who may well be teetering on the verge of stardom. (✆773-549-4140; www. metrochicago.com; 3730 N Clark St; ⊙box office noon-6pm Mon, to 8pm Tue-Sat; Ⓜ Red Line to Addison)

Annoyance Theatre COMEDY

10 ⭐ Map p82, C5

A Chicago improv mainstay for more than 25 years, the Annoyance masterminds naughty and absurd shows, often musicals such as *Tiny Fascists: A Boy Scout Musical*. Performances take place on two stages nightly. Susan Messing's Thursday-night session ($5) always provides good yuks. The little lobby bar has good, cheap microbrews on tap. (✆773-697-9693; www.theannoyance. com; 851 W Belmont Ave; Ⓜ Red, Brown, Purple Line to Belmont)

Shopping

Strange Cargo CLOTHING

11 🔒 Map p82, B3

This retro store stocks hipster wear, platform shoes, wigs and a mind-blowing array of kitschy T-shirts. Staff will iron on decals of Harry Caray, Mike Ditka, the Hancock Center or other local touchstones, as well as Obama, Smurfs and more – all supreme souvenirs. (✆773-327-8090; www.strangecargo.com; 3448 N Clark St; ⊙11am-6:30pm Mon-Fri, to 6pm Sat, to 5pm Sun; Ⓜ Red Line to Addison)

 Top Tip

Managing the Wrigleyville Crowds

If there's a Cubs game at Wrigley Field, plan on around 30,000 extra people joining you for a visit to the neighborhood. The trains and buses will be stuffed to capacity, traffic will be snarled, and bars and restaurants will be jam-packed. It can be fun...if that's your scene. If not, you might want to visit on a non-game day for a bit more elbow room.

Local Life
Mixing It Up in Andersonville & Uptown

Getting There

Ⓜ Red Line to Berwyn (six blocks east of Clark St) for Andersonville. Red Line to Lawrence for Green Mill.

🚌 Bus 22 travels along Clark St.

Andersonville is an old Swedish enclave, where timeworn European-tinged businesses mix with new foodie restaurants, antique shops; and gay and lesbian bars. Nearby Uptown is a whole different scene, with historic jazz houses such as the Green Mill (Al Capone's fave), along with the thriving eateries of 'Little Saigon.' Both areas are prime to stroll and to window-shop, eat and drink.

1 Hamburger Mary's

Campy **Hamburger Mary's** (☎773-784-6969; www.hamburgermarys.com/chicago; 5400 N Clark St; ☺11:30am-midnight Sun-Wed, to 1:30am Thu & Fri, to 2:30am Sat) is an LGBTQI spot that all of Andersonville hangs out at. It serves well-regarded burgers and weekend brunch in the downstairs restaurant, but the action's on the rowdy, booze-soaked patio.

2 Big Jones

Warm, sunny **Big Jones** (☎773-275-5725; www.bigjoneschicago.com; 5347 N Clark St; mains $17-23; ☺11am-9pm Mon-Thu, to 10pm Fri, from 9am Sat & Sun) puts 'southern heirloom cooking' on the menu. Residents flock in for chicken and dumplings, crawfish étouffée and shrimp and grits. The decadent, biscuit-laden brunch draws the biggest crowds.

3 Simon's

Open since 1934, **Simon's** (☎773-878-0894; 5210 N Clark St; ☺11am-2am Sun-Fri, to 3am Sat) is a dimly lit musicians' watering hole. The jukebox rocks an eclectic lineup ranging from Robert Gordon to Elastica to the Clash. In winter, in homage to its Swedish roots, Simon's serves *glogg* (spiced wine punch).

4 Woolly Mammoth

Woolly Mammoth Antiques & Oddities (☎773-989-3294; www.woollymammothchicago.com; 1513 W Foster Ave; ☺1-7pm Mon, from 3pm Tue, from noon Wed-Sun) is part morbid curiosity shop, part art installation. Creepy doll heads, a stuffed wallaby, jar of old dentures, a record book from an asylum – it's all here, and then some.

5 Hopleaf

A cozy, European-style tavern, **Hopleaf** (☎773-334-9851; www.hopleaf.com; 5148 N Clark St; mains $12-27; ☺noon-11pm Mon-Thu, to midnight Fri & Sat, to 10pm Sun) is a community favorite for its cashew-butter-and-figjam sandwich and house specialty of *frites* and ale-soaked mussels. It also pours 200 types of beers, emphasizing craft and Belgian suds.

6 Hot G Dog

Hot G Dog (☎773-209-3360; www.hotgdog.com; 5009 N Clark St; hot dogs $2.50-4; ☺10:30am-8pm Mon-Sat, to 4pm Sun) is the place to bite into, say, a chicken apple cranberry hotdog with whiskey cheese and pecans. It's also a fine place to try an ol' Chicago-style dog. The chefs formerly worked at Hot Doug's famed shop.

7 Nha Hang Viet Nam

Little **Nha Hang Viet Nam** (☎773-878-8895; 1032 W Argyle St; mains $7-13; ☺8:30am-10pm Wed-Mon) may not look like much from the outside, but it offers a huge menu of authentic, well-made dishes from the homeland. It's terrific for pho and clay-pot catfish.

8 Green Mill

The timeless **Green Mill** (☎773-878-5552; www.greenmilljazz.com; 4802 N Broadway; ☺noon-4am Mon-Fri, to 5am Sat, 11am-4am Sun) earned its notoriety as Al Capone's favorite speakeasy. Sit in one of the curved leather booths and feel his ghost urging you on to another martini. Local and national jazz artists perform nightly.

Explore

Wicker Park, Bucktown & Ukrainian Village

These three neighborhoods are hot property. Hipster record stores, thrift shops and cocktail lounges have shot up, though vintage Eastern European dive bars linger on many street corners. Wicker Park is the beating heart; Bucktown (a bit posher) and Ukrainian Village (a bit shabbier) flank it. The restaurant and rock-club scene is unparalleled in the city.

The Sights in a Day

☀ Have a Tex Mex breakfast at retro diner **Dove's Luncheonette** (p92), then get ready for a hipster shopping spree along Milwaukee and North Aves. Hot spots include **Reckless Records** (p96), **Quimby's** (p96) and **Una Mae's** (p96).

☀ For a change of pace, rise above the commerce by taking a walk on the **606 Trail** (p92). The city converted an old, elevated train track into a groovy walking path. It gives a great feel for the different neighborhoods it traverses.

🌙 So many choices for dinner: **Mana Food Bar** (p93) and **Big Star** (p93) are in the thick of it. **Ruxbin** (p92) and **Irazu** (p93) are a bit off the beaten path. For drinks, go highbrow with cocktails at the **Violet Hour** (p94). Or opt for a mellower, beer-fueled evening at **Map Room** (p95). You're spoiled for choice when it comes to indie-cool live music venues. The **Hideout** (p95) and **Empty Bottle** (p95) always have great shows.

 Best of Chicago

Eating
Dove's Luncheonette (p92)

Irazu (p93)

Ruxbin (p92)

Mana Food Bar (p93)

Handlebar (p94)

Flo (p94)

Live Music
Hideout (p95)

Empty Bottle (p95)

Drinking & Nightlife
Violet Hour (p94)

Shopping
Reckless Records (p96)

Quimby's (p96)

Dusty Groove (p97)

Una Mae's (p96)

Getting There

Ⓜ **El** Blue Line to Damen for Bucktown and northern Wicker Park; Blue Line to Division for southern Wicker Park; Blue Line to Chicago for Ukrainian Village.

🚌 **Bus** Bus 72 runs along North Ave; bus 49 along Western Ave; bus 66 along Chicago Ave.

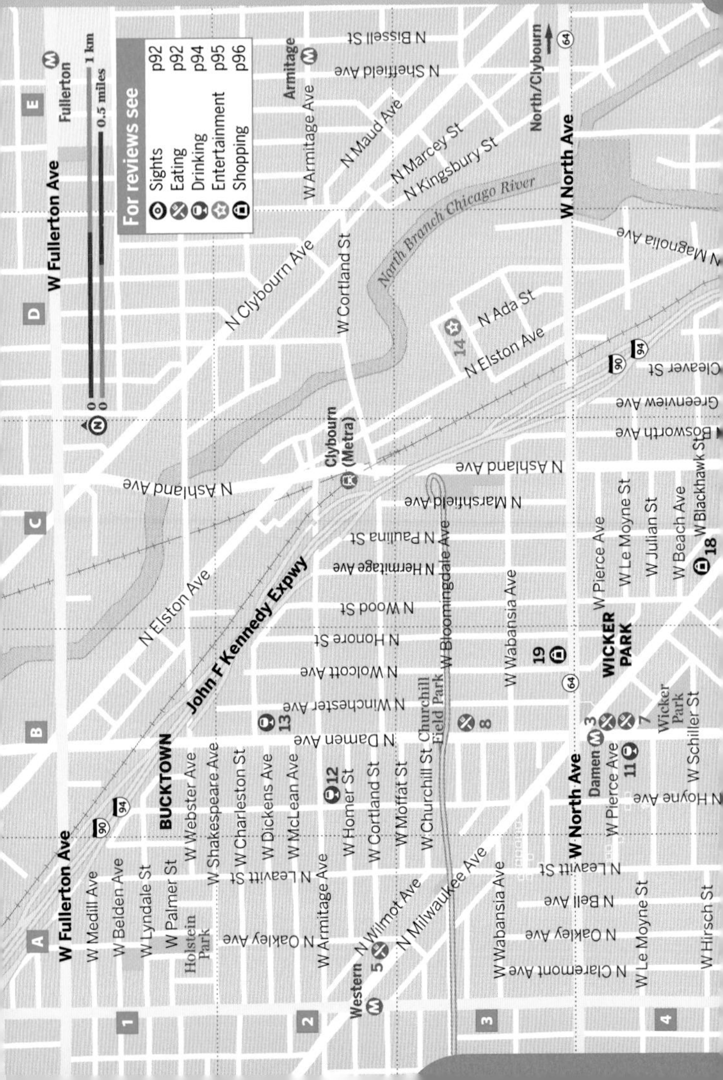

For reviews see
Sights p92
Eating p92
Drinking p94
Entertainment p95
Shopping p96
1 km
0.5 miles
A
B
C
D
E
1
2
3
4
W Fullerton Ave
Fullerton
Armitage
W Armitage Ave
N Bissell St
N Sheffield Ave
N Maud Ave
N Marcey St
N Kingsbury St
North/Clybourn
W North Ave
North Branch Chicago River
N Magnolia Ave
N Clybourn Ave
W Cortland St
N Ada St
N Elston Ave
Cleaver St
Greenview Ave
Bosworth Ave
N Ashland Ave
Clybourn (Metra)
N Marshfield Ave
N Paulina St
N Hermitage Ave
N Wood St
N Honore St
N Wolcott Ave
N Winchester Ave
N Damen Ave
John F Kennedy Expwy
N Elston Ave
BUCKTOWN
W Medill Ave
W Belden Ave
W Lyndale St
W Palmer St
Holstein Park
W Webster Ave
W Shakespeare Ave
W Charleston St
W Dickens Ave
W McLean Ave
W Homer St
W Cortland St
W Moffat St
W Churchill St
Churchill Field Park
W Bloomingdale Ave
W Wabansia Ave
W Pierce Ave
W Le Moyne St
W Julian St
W Beach Ave
W Blackhawk St
WICKER PARK
Wicker Park
Damen
W Schiller St
N Hoyne Ave
N Leavitt St
N Bell Ave
N Oakley Ave
N Claremont Ave
W Hirsch St
N Wilmot Ave
N Milwaukee Ave
Western
W Armitage Ave
W Wabansia Ave
W Le Moyne St
W North Ave
90
94
64
3
5
7
8
11
12
13
14
18
19

Sights

Intuit: The Center for Intuitive & Outsider Art GALLERY

1 ◎ Map p90, E7

Behold the museum-like collection of folk art, including watercolors by famed local Henry Darger. In the back room Intuit has recreated Darger's awesomely cluttered studio, complete with balls of twine, teetering stacks of old magazines and a Victrola phonograph. The gift shop carries groovy jewelry (such as pencil-eraser earrings) and art books. (☏312-243-9088; www.art.org; 756 N Milwaukee Ave; suggested donation $5; ◷11am-6pm Tue, Wed, Fri & Sat, to 7:30pm Thu, noon-5pm Sun; Ⓜ Blue Line to Chicago)

○ Local Life
606 Trail

Like NYC's High Line, Chicago's **606** (www.the606.org; ◷6am-11pm; Ⓜ Blue Line to Damen) is an urban-cool elevated path along an old train track. Bike or stroll past factories, smokestacks, clattering El trains and locals' backyard affairs for 2.7 miles between Wicker Park and Logan Square. It's a fascinating trek through Chicago's socioeconomic strata: moneyed at the east, becoming more industrial and immigrant to the west. The trail parallels Bloomingdale Ave, with access points every quarter mile.

Document Gallery GALLERY

2 ◎ Map p90, C6

Document organizes exhibitions of contemporary photography, film and media-based works by emerging artists. It shares its large space with three other galleries, and the stretch of Chicago Ave that it's on holds quite a few more art showrooms to boot. Mosey between 1400 and 2200 W Chicago Ave for further gallery explorations. (☏262-719-3500; www.documentspace.com; 1709 W Chicago Ave; ◷11am-6pm Wed-Sat; 🚌66; Ⓜ Blue Line to Chicago)

Eating

Dove's Luncheonette TEX-MEX $$

3 🍴 Map p90, B4

Grab a seat at the retro counter for Tex-Mex plates of pork-shoulder posole and shrimp-stuffed sweet-corn tamales. Dessert? It's pie, of course – maybe lemon cream or peach jalapeno, depending on what staff have baked that day. Soul music spins on a record player, tequila flows from the 70 bottles rattling behind the bar, and presto: all is right in the world. (☏773-645-4060; www.doveschicago.com; 1545 N Damen Ave; mains $13-19; ◷9am-9pm Mon-Thu, 8am-10pm Fri & Sat, 8am-9pm Sun; Ⓜ Blue Line to Damen)

Ruxbin AMERICAN $$$

4 🍴 Map p90, C6

The passion of the Kim family, who run pocket-sized Ruxbin, is evident in everything from the mod, slate-and-wood decor to the artfully prepared flavors on the ever-changing, hyper-local menu. Pick five dishes from the week's list – say, cider-glazed pork belly or thyme-and-morel-plumped ravioli – to share with the table. You can downsize to three dishes on Wednesday, Thursday and Sunday. BYOB. (📞312-624-8509; www.ruxbinchicago.com; 851 N Ashland Ave; 3-/5-dish menu $55/85; ⏱6-10pm Wed & Thu, from 5:30 Fri-Sun; Ⓜ Blue Line to Division)

Irazu   LATIN AMERICAN $

5 ✕ Map p90, A2

Chicago's unassuming lone Costa Rican eatery turns out burritos bursting with chicken, black beans and fresh avocado, and sandwiches dressed in a heavenly, spicy-sweet vegetable sauce. Wash them down with an *avena* (a slurpable oatmeal milkshake). For breakfast, the *arroz con huevos* (peppery eggs scrambled into rice) relieves hangovers. Irazu is BYOB with no corkage fee. Cash only. (📞773-252-5687; www.irazuchicago.com; 1865 N Milwaukee Ave; mains $11-15; ⏱11:30am-9:30pm Mon-Sat; Ⓜ Blue Line to Western)

Mana Food Bar   VEGETARIAN $$

6 ✕ Map p90, C5

What's unique here is the focus on creating global dishes without using fake meats. So you won't find soy chorizo or tempeh reubens, but rather multi-ethnic veggie dishes from the likes of Japan, Korea, Italy and the American Southwest. Beer, smoothies and sake cocktails help wash it down. This eatery

Bike riders on the 606 trail

buzzes, so reserve ahead or prepare to wait. (📞773-342-1742; www.manafoodbar.com; 1742 W Division St; small plates $7-10; ⏱5:30-10pm Mon-Thu, to 11pm Fri, noon-11pm Sat, 5-9pm Sun; 🌿; Ⓜ Blue Line to Division)

Big Star   MEXICAN $

7 ✕ Map p90, B4

Once a filling station, it's now a taco-serving honky-tonk bar helmed by big-name Chicago chef Paul Kahan. So goes gentrification in Wicker Park. The place gets packed, but damn, those tacos are worth the wait – pork belly in tomato-*guajillo* chili sauce and mole-spiced carrots drizzled with date-infused yogurt accompany the specialty whiskey list. (📞773-235-4039; www.bigstarchicago.com; 1531 N Damen Ave;

tacos $3-4; ⏱11:30am-1:30am Sun-Fri, to 2:30am Sat; Ⓜ Blue Line to Damen)

Mindy's Hot Chocolate

AMERICAN $$

8 Map p90, B3

'Come for dessert, stay for dinner' might be the motto at this mod restaurant helmed by renowned pastry chef Mindy Segal. With nine kinds of hot chocolate available (they're like dipping your mug into Willy Wonka's chocolate river), along with cakes, cookies and mini brioche doughnuts, you may forget to order the caramel-roasted chicken, crab spaghetti and other seasonally changing mains on offer. It's a great date night place. (☎773-489-1747; www.hotchocolatechicago.com; 1747 N Damen Ave; mains $18-25; ⏱5:30-10pm Tue, 11:30am-2pm & 5:30-10pm Wed & Thu, to

Ｑ Local Life
Handlebar
The cult of the bike messenger runs strong in Chicago, and clamorous **Handlebar** (Map p91, A4; ☎773-384-9546; www.handlebarchicago.com; 2311 W North Ave; mains $11-15; ⏱10am-midnight Mon-Fri, from 9am Sat & Sun; 🍴; Ⓜ Blue Line to Damen) is where the tattooed couriers and other bike-loving locals hang out. They come for the strong, microbrew-centric beer list, vegetarian-friendly food (including West African groundnut stew and fried avocado tacos) and festive back beer garden.

midnight Fri, 10am-2pm & 5:30pm-midnight Sat, to 10pm Sun; Ⓜ Blue Line to Damen)

Flo

MEXICAN $

9 Map p90, D6

Think you've had a good breakfast burrito before? Not until you've eaten here. The Southwestern-bent dishes and jovial staff draw hordes of late-rising neighborhood hipsters on the weekend. Tart, potent margaritas and fish tacos take over after dark, but the breakfast foods are the main draw. (☎312-243-0477; www.flochicago.com; 1434 W Chicago Ave; mains $12-16; ⏱8:30am-10pm Tue-Thu, 8:30am-11pm Fri, 9am-11pm Sat, 9am-3pm Sun; Ⓜ Blue Line to Chicago)

Drinking

Matchbox

BAR

10 Map p90, E6

Lawyers, artists and bums all squeeze in for retro cocktails. It's as small as – you got it – a matchbox, with about 10 bar stools; everyone else stands against the back wall. Barkeeps make the drinks from scratch. Favorites include the pisco sour and the ginger gimlet, ladled from an amber vat of homemade ginger-infused vodka. (☎312-666-9292; 770 N Milwaukee Ave; ⏱4pm-2am Mon-Thu, from 3pm Fri-Sun; Ⓜ Blue Line to Chicago)

Violet Hour

COCKTAIL BAR

11 Map p90, B4

This nouveau speakeasy isn't marked, so look for the mural-slathered, wood-paneled building and the door topped by a yellow lightbulb. Inside, high-backed booths, chandeliers and long velvet drapes provide the backdrop to elaborately engineered cocktails that the Beard Awards deemed best in the US. The Pajama Boy (bourbon and pear brandy) shows why. As highbrow as it sounds, Violet Hour is welcoming and accessible. (☑773-252-1500; www.theviolethour.com; 1520 N Damen Ave; ⊗6pm-2am Sun-Fri, to 3am Sat; Ⓜ Blue Line to Damen)

Map Room

BAR

 12 Map p90, B2

At this map- and globe-filled 'travelers' tavern,' artsy types sip coffee by day and suds from the 200-strong beer list by night. Board games and old issues of *National Geographic* are within reach for entertainment. (☑773-252-7636; www.maproom.com; 1949 N Hoyne Ave; ⊗6:30am-2am Mon-Fri, 7:30am-3am Sat, 11am-2am Sun; 🛜; Ⓜ Blue Line to Western)

Danny's

BAR

 13 Map p90, B2

Danny's comfortably dim and dog-eared ambience is perfect for conversations over a pint early on and then DJs arrive to stoke the dance party as the evening progresses. The groovy spot is more like a house than a bar, filled with 20- and 30-somethings getting their moves on. Cash only. (☑773-489-6457; 1951 W Dickens Ave; ⊗7pm-2am Sun-Fri, to 3am Sat; Ⓜ Blue Line to Damen)

◯ Local Life

Happy Village

Happy Village (Map p91, B5; 1059 N Wolcott Ave; ⊗4pm-2am Mon-Fri, noon-3am Sat, noon-2am Sun; Ⓜ Blue Line to Division) may well be the jolliest bar in the neighborhood. Unapologetically divey, with cheap, non-craft beer, it earns smiles for its fierce table-tennis matches, starry vine-covered patio and strolling tamale vendor who seems to appear just when you need him most. Cash only.

Entertainment

Hideout

LIVE MUSIC

14 Map p90, D3

Hidden behind a factory at the edge of Bucktown, this two-room lodge of indie rock and alt-country is well worth seeking out. The owners have nursed an outsider, underground vibe, and the place feels like your grandma's rumpus room. Music and other events (talk shows, literary readings etc) take place nightly. (☑773-227-4433; www.hideoutchicago.com; 1354 W Wabansia Ave; tickets $5-15; ⊗5pm-2am Mon & Tue, from 4pm Wed-Fri, 7pm-3am Sat, hours vary Sun; 🚌72)

Empty Bottle

LIVE MUSIC

15 Map p90, A5

Chicago's music insiders fawn over the Empty Bottle, the city's scruffy, go-to club for edgy indie rock, jazz and other beats. Monday's show is often a freebie by a couple of up-and-coming bands.

Cheap beer, a photo booth and good graffiti-reading in the bathrooms add to the dive-bar fun. (☎773-276-3600; www.emptybottle.com; 1035 N Western Ave; ⏱5pm-2am Mon-Wed, from 3pm Thu & Fri, from 11am Sat & Sun; 🚌49)

Chopin Theatre   THEATER

16 Map p90, C5

Looking for a tasty slice of fringe theater? Something oddball, thought-provoking or just plain silly? Chopin is the place. The city's best itinerant companies, such as **House Theatre** (☎773-769-3832; www.thehousetheatre.com) and Theater Oobleck, often turn up here. (☎773-278-1500; www.chopintheatre.com; 1543 W Division St; 🅼Blue Line to Division)

Phyllis' Musical Inn   LIVE MUSIC

17 Map p90, C5

One of the all-time great dives, this former Polish polka bar features scrappy

> ### Local Life
> #### Una Mae's
> The half-mile stretch of Milwaukee Ave between North and Paulina Aves holds several vintage and thrift shops. **Una Mae's** (Map p91, B4; ☎773-276-7002; www.unamaeschicago.com; 1528 N Milwaukee Ave; ⏱noon-8pm Mon-Fri, 11am-8pm Sat, noon-7pm Sun; 🅼Blue Line to Damen) is a fine spot to browse for a pillbox hat or velvet-and-lace dress. It also has a collection of new, cool-cat designer duds and accessories for both men and women.

up-and-coming bands nightly. It's hit or miss for quality, but you've got to applaud them for taking a chance. If you don't like the sound, you can always slip outside to the bar's basketball court for relief. Cheap brewskis to boot. (☎773-486-9862; 1800 W Division St; ⏱4pm-2am Mon-Fri, from 3pm Sat, from 2pm Sun; 🅼Blue Line to Division)

Shopping

Reckless Records   MUSIC

18 Map p90, C4

Chicago's best indie-rock record and CD emporium allows you to listen to everything before you buy. It's certainly the place to get your finger on the pulse of the local, au courant underground scene. There's plenty of elbow room in the big, sunny space, which makes for happy hunting through the new and used bins. Reasonable prices too. (☎773-235-3727; 1379 N Milwaukee Ave; ⏱10am-10pm Mon-Sat, to 8pm Sun; 🅼Blue Line to Damen)

Quimby's   BOOKS

19 Map p90, B3

The epicenter of Chicago's comic and zine worlds, Quimby's is one of the linchpins of underground culture in the city. Here you can find everything from crayon-powered punk-rock manifestos to slickly produced graphic novels. It's a groovy place for cheeky literary souvenirs and bizarro readings. (☎773-342-0910; www.quimbys.

Unison Home

com; 1854 W North Ave; ⊙noon-9pm Mon-Thu, to 10pm Fri, 11am-10pm Sat, noon-7pm Sun; MBlue Line to Damen)

Dusty Groove
MUSIC

20 🔒 Map p90, C5

Old-school soul, Brazilian beats, Hungarian disco, bass-stabbing hip-hop – if it's funky, Dusty Groove (which also has its own record label) stocks it. Flip through stacks of vinyl, or get lost amid the tidy shop's CDs. Be sure to check out the bargain basement, as well as the 3rd floor's funky, contemporary art gallery. (📞773-342-5800; www.dustygroove.com; 1120 N Ashland Ave; ⊙10am-8pm; MBlue Line to Division)

Unison Home
HOMEWARES

21 🔒 Map p90, B5

Packed with boldly patterned bedding, smart storage solutions and striking decor, this beautifully curated store is a place you wander into and immediately want to dwell inside. It's the public face of Unison, a Chicago-based company specializing in modern textiles – napkins, tablecloths, throw pillows and more – and distinctive home goods by independent artists and designers from Chicago, Japan and Scandinavia. (📞773-227-3180; www.unisonhome.com; 1911 W Division St; ⊙11am-7pm Mon-Fri, 10am-6pm Sat, noon-6pm Sun; MBlue Line to Division)

Local Life
A Night Out in Logan Square

Getting There

M Blue Line to Logan Square (for places north of Fullerton Ave) or California (for places south of Fullerton).

Logan Square has become the 'it' hood for new and cool. But it's also refreshingly low-key, as it remains off the beaten path. Street-art displays, unassuming Michelin-starred taverns and dive bars chock-full of local color dot the leafy boulevards. Try to arrive early in the evening to take advantage of the shops and galleries.

❶ Revolution Brewing

Raise your fist to **Revolution** (☎773-227-2739; www.revbrew.com; 2323 N Milwaukee Ave; ⏰11am-1am Mon-Fri, 10am-1am Sat, 10am-11pm Sun), a big, buzzy, industrial-chic brewpub that serves as the neighborhood clubhouse. The brewmaster led the way for Chicago's craft-beer scene, and his suds are top notch. The haute pub grub includes arugula-and-mozzarella pizza and bacon-fat popcorn with fried sage.

❷ Cole's

Cole's (☎773-276-5802; www.coleschicago.com; 2338 N Milwaukee Ave; ⏰5:30pm-2am Mon-Fri, from 4pm Sat & Sun) is a dive bar with nifty free entertainment. Scenesters flockin to shoot pool and swill Midwest microbrews in the neon-bathed front room. Then they head to the backroom stage where bands and DJs do their thing. On Wednesday the comedy open mic takes over.

❸ Galerie F

Galerie F (☎872-817-7067; www.galerief.com; 2415 N Milwaukee Ave; ⏰11am-6pm Tue-Sun) is exactly the type of laid-back, ubercool gallery you'd expect to find in Logan Square. It specializes in rock-and-roll gig posters, printmaking and street art. Walk into the bright, open space and browse. The vibe is totally welcoming.

❹ Whistler

Hometown indie bands, jazz combos and DJs rock wee, arty **Whistler** (☎773-227-3530; www.whistlerchicago.com; 2421 N Milwaukee Ave; ⏰6pm-2am Mon-Thu,

5pm-2am Fri-Sun) most nights. There's never a cover charge, but you'd be a shmuck if you didn't order at least one of the swanky cocktails to keep the scene going. It's also a gallery: the front window showcases local artists' work.

❺ Wolfbait & B-girls

Old ironing boards serve as display tables; tape measures, scissors and other designers' tools hang from vintage hooks. You get that crafting feeling as soon as you walk in, and indeed, **Wolfbait & B-girls** (☎312-698-8685; www.wolfbaitchicago.com; 3131 W Logan Blvd; ⏰10am-7pm Mon-Sat, to 4pm Sun) sells the handmade wares (dresses, handbags and jewelry) of local indie designers.

❻ Longman & Eagle

It's hard to say whether shabby-chic tavern **Longman & Eagle** (☎773-276-7110; www.longmanandeagle.com; 2657 N Kedzie Ave; mains $16-30; ⏰9am-2am Sun-Fri, to 3am Sat) is better for eating or drinking. Let's say eating, since it earned a Michelin star for its beautifully cooked comfort foods such as wild-boar sloppy joes; and fried chicken and duck fat biscuits.

❼ Lost Lake

Hipsters love a good tiki bar, so **Lost Lake** (☎773-293-6048; www.lostlaketiki.com; 3154 W Diversey Ave; ⏰4pm-2am Sun-Fri, to 3am Sat) popped up in 2015 to meet the need. Take a seat under the bamboo roof, by the banana leaf wallpaper, and swirl a Mystery Gardenia or other tropical drink made from one of the 275 rums on offer.

Explore

Near West Side & Pilsen

The Near West Side covers a large swath including Greektown and the booming West Loop, which was once the city's meatpacking district. It now buzzes with hot-chef restaurants and on-trend bars. Development continues here big-time. In Pilsen, Mexican culture mixes with Chicago's bohemian underground, and colorful murals, taquerias and cafes result.

The Sights in a Day

☀ A tough breakfast decision awaits: **Lou Mitchell's** (p106) has Route 66 ambience going for it; **Meli Cafe** (p108) has peach crepes in Greektown. If it's the last weekend of the month **Randolph Street Market** (p111) is a big to-do.

☀ Take the train to Pilsen. The **National Museum of Mexican Art** (p106) has terrific free exhibits, while 18th St rolls out groovy shops such as **Modern Cooperative** (p110) and **Knee Deep Vintage** (p111). They share the sidewalk with **Don Pedro Carnitas** (p108), **La Catrina Cafe** (p109) and other Mexican spots, as well as hipster havens such as **Pleasant House Pub** (p109).

☾ The West Loop is one of Chicago's richest zones for dinner. Try for reservations at **Roister** (p106), **Girl & the Goat** (p107) or **Little Goat** (p106), or get in line at **Au Cheval** (p107). Bubbly drinks at **RM Champagne Salon** (p109) is a fine finale.

For a local's day in the West Loop, see p102.

 Local Life

West Loop Wander (p102)

 Best of Chicago

Eating
Pleasant House Pub (p109)

Girl & the Goat (p107)

Publican Quality Meats (p103)

Drinking & Nightlife
RM Champagne Salon (p109)

Museums & Galleries
National Museum of Mexican Art (p106)

Mars Gallery (p102)

Shopping
Knee Deep Vintage (p111)

For Kids
Lou Mitchell's (p106)

Getting There

Ⓜ **El** Pink Line to 18th St for Pilsen; Green, Pink Line to Morgan or Clinton for West Loop; Blue Line to UIC-Halsted for Greektown.

🚍 **Bus** For United Center, buses 19 (game-day express) and 20 run along Madison St. Number 8 travels along Halsted St through Greektown and Pilsen.

Local Life
West Loop Wander

The West Loop has exploded in the last few years with hotshot restaurants and condos carved from old meatpacking warehouses. While a few bloody-apron-clad workers remain, these days you're more likely to run into a Google employee toting a latte as you traverse the galleries and mega-stylish eateries inhabiting the industrial buildings.

1 Cool Cat Gallery

Pop-art-filled **Mars Gallery** (☎312-226-7808; www.marsgallery.com; 1139 W Fulton Market; ⊘noon-6pm Wed & Fri, to 7pm Thu, 11am-5pm Sat; ⓜGreen, Pink Line to Morgan) is pure fun, from the plaid-tie-wearing cat who roams the premises (he's the assistant manager, according to the sign) to the building's offbeat history (it was an egg factory, then a club where the Ramones played). Weird bonus: it sits atop an energy vortex.

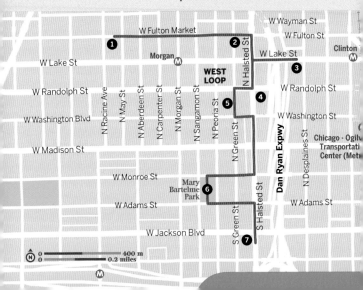

❷ Meat Treat

Neighborhood dwellers come to **Publican Quality Meats** (☎312-445-8977; www.publicanqualitymeats.com; 825 W Fulton Market; mains $11-14; ⊗8am-6pm Mon-Fri, 9am-6pm Sat, 9am-5pm Sun; Ⓜ Green, Pink Line to Morgan) for its supply of smoked chorizo and maple breakfast sausage. Then they pull up a chair in the small restaurant in the back and linger over beer and artisanal sandwiches. In summer the crowd spills out to street-side tables.

❸ Do-Good Books

Thrifty hipsters in need of a good read browse the gently used stacks at **Open Books** (☎312-475-1355; www.open-books.org; 651 W Lake St; ⊗9am-7pm Mon-Sat, noon-6pm Sun; ▣; Ⓜ Green, Pink Line to Clinton). Hours slip by as they scan shelves that hold *Little House on the Prairie* next to Gwyneth Paltrow's latest cookbook next to a 1987 guidebook to Alaska. All proceeds go toward the nonprofit shop's literacy programs for local kids.

❹ Historic Suds

Haymarket Pub & Brewery (☎312-638-0700; www.haymarketbrewing.com; 737 W Randolph St; ⊗11am-2am Sun-Fri, to 3am Sat; Ⓜ Green, Pink Line to Clinton) provides a nice dose of local history. It's located near where the 1886 Haymarket labor riot took place, and the brewery's suds often have affiliated names, such as the Mathias Imperial IPA (named after the first police officer to die in the melee) and the Speakerswagon Pilsner.

❺ Artful Coffee

West Loop workers at Google, Uber and the district's other tech companies need to stay caffeinated, and **Sawada Coffee** (☎312-754-0431; http://sawadacoffee.com; 112 N Green St; ⊗8am-5pm; ▣; Ⓜ Green, Pink Line to Morgan) provides the requisite lattes. The signature one is made with matcha (green tea powder) and poured exquisitely. Sawada's wi-fi, epicurean doughnuts and cozy, rustic-chic interior invite lingering.

❻ Park Stroll

The neighborhood's stroller-pushing families and dog-walking hipsters get their exercise in **Mary Bartelme Park** (115 S Sangamon St; Ⓜ Blue Line to UIC-Halsted). Five off-kilter stainless-steel arches form the gateway in; kids play in the mist that the sculptures release in summer. Grassy mounds dot the park and provide good lookout points to view the Willis Tower rising in the distance.

❼ Greek Delights

Chicago's small but busy Greektown centers on Halsted St. Residents head to **Artopolis Bakery & Cafe** (☎312-559-9000; www.artopolischicago.com; 306 S Halsted St; mains $10-17; ⊗9am-midnight Mon-Thu, to 1am Fri & Sat, 10am-11pm Sun; Ⓜ Blue Line to UIC-Halsted) for classics such as baklava and spinach-and-feta pies. The cafe-bar opens onto the street, with wine-laden tables along the front.

105

For reviews see
◉ Sights p106
☆ Eating p106
◉ Drinking p109
☆ Entertainment p110
◉ Shopping p110

0   500 m
0   0.25 miles

W 14th Pl
W 15th St
S Clinton St
S Jefferson St
W 14th St
W 15th St
W 16th St
W 18th St
S Jefferson St
W Cermak Rd

Dan Ryan Expwy

S Halsted St
Halsted St (Metra)
W 16th St
W 18th St
W 19th St
S Canal Port Ave
S Peoria St
13

S Racine Ave
W Maxwell St
W 14th Pl
W 14th St
W 16th St
W 18th St
S Cullerton St
W Cullerton St
S Morgan St
12
6
S Carpenter St
S May St
W 21st St

PILSEN
15
9
S Allport St
S Blue Island Ave
S Racine Ave
S Throop St

South Branch Chicago River

W 15th St
18
S Laflin St
S Loomis St
S Laflin St

W Washburne Ave
W 13th St
W Hastings St
W 14th St
W 16th St
S Ashland Ave
S Paulina St
18th St
W 18th Pl
W Cullerton St
W Cermak Rd
S Paulina St

S Wolcott Ave
W 13th St
W 14th St
Addams Park
W 17th St
W 18th St
Harrison Park
1
National Museum of Mexican Art
W 19th St
W 21st St
W 21st Pl
Hoyne
W 22nd Pl
S Wood St
S Blue Island Ave
S Wolcott Ave
W Cermak Rd

A   B   C   D   E

5   6   7   8

Sights

National Museum of Mexican Art

MUSEUM

1 ◎ Map p104, A6

Founded in 1982, this vibrant museum – the largest Latino arts institution in the US – has become one of the city's best. The vivid permanent collection sums up 1000 years of Mexican art and culture through classical paintings, shining gold altars, skeleton-rich folk art, beadwork and much more. (☑312-738-1503; www.nationalmuseumofmexicanart.org; 1852 W 19th St; admission free; ⊙10am-5pm Tue-Sun; ⓂPink Line to 18th St)

Eating

Little Goat

DINER $$

Top Chef winner Stephanie Izard opened this diner (see 5 ⊗ Map p104, D1) for the foodie masses across the street from her ever-booked main restaurant, Girl & the Goat (p107). Scooch into a vintage booth and order off the all-day breakfast menu. Better yet, try lunch and dinner favorites such as the goat sloppy joe with rosemary slaw or pork belly on scallion pancakes. Izard's flavor combinations rule. (☑312-888-3455; www.littlegoatchicago.com; 820 W Randolph St; mains $10-19; ⊙7am-10pm Sun-Thu, to midnight Fri & Sat; ☎⊿; ⓂGreen, Pink Line to Morgan)

Lou Mitchell's

BREAKFAST $

2 ⊗ Map p104, E2

A relic of Route 66, Lou's brings in elbow-to-elbow locals and tourists for breakfast. The old-school waitresses deliver fluffy omelets that hang off the plate and thick-cut French toast with a jug of syrup. They call you 'honey' and fill your coffee cup endlessly. There's often a queue to get in, but free doughnut holes and Milk Duds help ease the wait. (☑312-939-3111; www.loumitchellsrestaurant.com; 565 W Jackson Blvd; mains $9-14; ⊙5:30am-3pm Mon, to 4pm Tue-Fri, 7am-4pm Sat, to 3pm Sun; ﬁ; ⓂBlue Line to Clinton)

Roister

AMERICAN $$$

3 ⊗ Map p104, D1

Roister lets you eat the food of molecular gastronomist Grant Achatz (the chef of three-Michelin-star Alinea; p74)) on the cheap. Here he cooks wild riffs on comfort foods while a rip-roaring rock soundtrack blasts. Dishes change and defy easy description – like the 'whole chicken' served with thighs fried, breast roasted and the rest melded into a chicken salad – but they're all rich and playful. Reserve ahead. (www.roisterrestaurant.com; 951 W Fulton Market; mains $28-32; ⊙11:45am-2pm & 5-10:30pm Mon-Thu, to 11pm Fri, 11:30am-3pm & 5-11pm Sat, to 10:30pm Sun; ⓂGreen, Pink Line to Morgan)

KIM KARPELES/ALAMY STOCK PHOTO ©

Mural of Our Lady of Guadalupe, Hispanic Pilsen neighborhood

Girl & the Goat

AMERICAN $$$

4 Map p104, D1

Stephanie Izard's flagship restaurant rocks. The soaring ceilings, polished wood tables and cartoon-y art on the walls offer a convivial atmosphere where local beer and housemade wine hit the tables, along with unique small plates such as catfish with pickled persimmons. Reservations are difficult; try for walk-in seats before 5pm or see if anything opens up at the bar. (📞312-492-6262; www.girlandthegoat.com; 809 W Randolph St; small plates $9-16; 🕓4:30-11pm Sun-Thu, to midnight Fri & Sat; 🍴; MGreen, Pink Line to Morgan)

Au Cheval

AMERICAN $$

5 Map p104, D1

People go crazy over Au Cheval's cheeseburger. It drips with a runny fried egg, melty cheddar and tangy dijonnaise, all stuffed into a bun fluffy enough to unhinge your jaw. *Bon Appetit* crowned it America's best burger, and the little diner has been mobbed since. No reservations, so prepare to wait (best done at the neighboring bar; staff will text when your table is ready). (📞312-929-4580; www.auchevalchicago.com; 800 W Randolph St; mains $12-19; 🕓11am-1am Mon-Sat, 10am-midnight Sun; MGreen, Pink Line to Morgan)

Top Tip

16th Street Murals

Pilsen is famous for its murals, which splash across churches, schools and cafes throughout the neighborhood. The 16th Street railroad embankment unfurls a particularly rich vein, with 50 works by local and international artists adorning a 1.5-mile stretch between Wood and Halsted Sts. The Pink Line train to 18th Street gets you within a few blocks of the strip's western end. The Divvy bike-share station outside of the El depot (on Paulina St) makes a mural-browsing trip even easier.

Don Pedro Carnitas
MEXICAN $

 6 Map p104, D6

At this no-frills meat den, a man with a machete salutes you at the front counter. He awaits your command to hack off pork pieces and then wraps the thick chunks with onion and cilantro in a fresh tortilla. You then devour the taco at the tables in back. Goat stew and tripe add to the carnivorous menu. Cash only. (1113 W 18th St; tacos $1.50-2; ⏰6am-6pm Mon-Fri, 5am-5pm Sat, 5am-3pm Sun; ⓜPink Line to 18th)

Avec
MEDITERRANEAN $$

7 Map p104, E1

Feeling social? This happening spot gives diners a chance to rub elbows at eight-person communal tables. The mini room looks a heck of a lot like a Finnish sauna and fills with noisy chatter as stylish urbanites pile in. The bacon-wrapped dates are the menu's must-try; the paella and the sausage and mint-pesto calzone are other standouts, though the menu changes regularly. (☎312-377-2002; www.avecrestaurant.com; 615 W Randolph St; mains $18-28; ⏰11:30am-2pm & 3:30pm-midnight Mon-Fri, 3:30pm-1am Sat, 10am-2pm & 3:30pm-midnight Sun; ⓜGreen, Pink Line to Clinton)

Meli Cafe
BREAKFAST $

8 Map p104, E2

Meli is the Greek word for 'honey,' and it's apt for this sweet breakfast spot. Cage-free eggs served over a bed of potatoes, kale-and-feta omelets, peach crepes and the decadent French toast (made from challah bread dipped in vanilla-bean custard) start the day off right. Meli has a few outposts around town. (☎312-454-0748; www.melicafe.com; 301 S Halsted St; mains $12-16; ⏰7am-3pm; ⓜBlue Line to UIC-Halsted)

Dusek's
GASTROPUB $$$

9 Map p104, C6

Pilsen's hipsters gather under the pressed-tin ceiling of this gastropub to fork into the ever-changing menu of beer-inspired dishes, such as beer-battered soft-shell crab or dark-lager-roasted duck. The eatery shares its historic building (modeled on Prague's opera house) with an indie-band concert hall (p110) and basement cocktail bar. (☎312-526-3851; www.dusekschicago.com; 1227 W 18th St; mains $18-30; ⏲11am-1am Mon-Fri, 9am-1am Sat & Sun; Ⓜ Pink Line to 18th St)

Drinking

RM Champagne Salon BAR

10 Map p104, D1

This West Loop spot is a twinkling-light charmer for bubbles. Score a table in the cobblestoned courtyard and you'll feel transported to Paris. (☎312-243-1199; www.rmchampagnesalon.com; 116 N Green St; ⏲5pm-midnight Mon-Thu, to 2am Fri & Sat, to 11pm Sun; Ⓜ Green, Pink Line to Morgan)

Goose Island Brewery BREWERY

11 Map p104, A1

Goose Island – Chicago's first craft brewer, launched in 1988 – is now owned by Anheuser-Busch InBev, so technically it's no longer a craft brewer. But it still acts like one, making excellent small-batch beers at this facility. The swanky mod-industrial taproom pours nine or so varieties; bring your own food to accompany them. Hour-long tours ($12) are available if you reserve in advance. (www.gooseisland.com; 1800 W Fulton St; ⏲2-8pm Thu & Fri, noon-6pm Sat & Sun; Ⓜ Green, Pink Line to Ashland)

La Catrina Cafe CAFE

12 Map p104, D6

Activists, artists and students congregate here for the roomy window seats, bottomless cups of coffee and funky art exhibitions. It's a come-one come-all kind of spot, prime for a Mexican hot chocolate and Frida Kahlo–face cookie. A colorful mural marks the entrance. (☎312-532-6817; 1011 W 18th St; ⏲7am-9pm Mon-Fri, 8am-6pm Sat & Sun; ⚲; Ⓜ Pink Line to 18th St)

Skylark BAR

13 Map p104, E7

The Skylark is a bastion for artsy drunkards, who slouch into big booths sipping on strong drinks and eyeing the long room. They

---

 Local Life

Pleasant House Pub

Join the neighborhood folks at **Pleasant House Pub** (Map p105, E7; ☎773-523-7437; www.facebook.com/pleasanthousepub; 2119 S Halsted St; mains $8-10; ⏲7am-10pm Tue-Thu, to midnight Fri, 10am-midnight Sat, to 10pm Sun; ⚲; 🚌8), which bakes tall, fluffy, savory pies. Flavors include chicken and chutney, steak and ale, or kale and mushroom, made with produce the chefs grow themselves. The pub also serves its own beers (brewed off site). Friday is a good day to visit, when there's a fish fry.

play pinball, snap pics in the photo booth and scarf down the kitchen's awesome tater tots. It's a good stop after the Pilsen gallery hop (a free arts event run by galleries, shops and studios). Cash only. (☏312-948-5275; www.skylarkchicago.com; 2149 S Halsted St; ◷4pm-2am Sun-Fri, to 3am Sat; 🛜; 🚌8)

2Fun Chinese
COCKTAIL BAR

14 | Map p104, D1

This dimly lit yet lively cocktail lounge, located above stylish Sichuan restaurant WonFun Chinese, features karaoke, cocktails and a dim sum cart. Some beverages use sorghum-based baijiu, China's most popular spirit, such as the Shanghai Sky, which also includes mezcal and lemon ($12). (☏312-877-5967; www.funfunchinese.com; 905 W Randolph St, 2nd fl; ◷5pm-2am Tue-Fri, to 3am Sat; Ⓜ Green, Pink Line to Morgan)

Entertainment

Thalia Hall
LIVE MUSIC

15 | Map p104, C6

This venue hosts a cool-cat slate of rock, alt-country, jazz and metal in an ornate 1892 hall patterned after Prague's opera house. A gastropub (p108) on the 1st floor, cocktail bar in the basement and punk piano saloon in the adjacent carriage house invite lingering before and after shows. (☏312-526-3851; www.thaliahallchicago.com; 1807 S Allport St; Ⓜ Pink Line to 18th St)

Chicago Blackhawks
HOCKEY

16 | Map p104, A2

The Hawks skate at **United Center** (☏312-455-4650; www.unitedcenter.com; 1901 W Madison St; 🚌19 or 20). Tickets have become difficult to get, with lots of sellouts since the team's Stanley Cup wins (in 2010, 2013 and 2015). Be sure to arrive in time for the national anthem at the game's start. The raucous, ear-splitting rendition is a tradition. Express bus number 19 plies Madison St on game days. (☏312-455-7000; www.nhl.com/blackhawks; 1901 W Madison St; 🚌19, 20)

Chicago Bulls
BASKETBALL

17 | Map p104, A2

They may not be the mythical champions of yore, but the Bulls still draw good crowds to its United Center home base. Tickets are available through the United Center box office – located in the glass atrium on the building's eastern side, along with the famed, slam-dunking Michael Jordan statue – and at Ticketmaster outlets. (☏312-455-4000; www.nba.com/bulls; 1901 W Madison St; 🚌19, 20)

Shopping

Modern Cooperative
VINTAGE

ModCo (see 15 | Map p104, C6) carries a terrific selection of mid-century modern furniture from the 1960s and '70s, as well as artworks, jewelry, pillows and bags from current local designers.

2Fun Chinese is located above WonFun Chinese (pictured)

It is located inside Pilsen's historic Thalia Hall building. The shop has another outpost in Hyde Park. (📞312-226-8525; www.moderncooperative.com; 1215 W 18th St; ⏱11am-7pm Wed-Fri, to 6pm Sat & Sun; Ⓜ Pink Line to 18th St)

Knee Deep Vintage VINTAGE

18 🔒 Map p104, C6

Knee Deep offers a trove of vintage clothing (for men and women), housewares and vinyl. There's a sale the second Friday of every month, with items slashed 25% to 50%; it's held in conjunction with the local gallery hop (a free event run by galleries, shops and studios), starting at 6pm. (📞312-850-2510; www.kneedeepvintage. com; 1425 W 18th St; ⏱noon-7pm Mon-Thu, 11am-8pm Fri & Sat, noon-6pm Sun; Ⓜ Pink Line to 18th St)

Randolph Street Market MARKET

19 🔒 Map p104, C1

This market, which styles itself on London's Portobello Market, has become quite the to-do in town. It takes place inside the beaux-arts Plumbers Hall, where more than 200 antique dealers hock collectibles, costume jewelry, furniture, books, Turkish rugs and pinball machines. (www.randolphstreetmarket.com; 1340 W Washington Blvd; $10; ⏱10am-5pm Sat & Sun, last weekend of the month Feb-Dec; Ⓜ Green, Pink Line to Ashland)

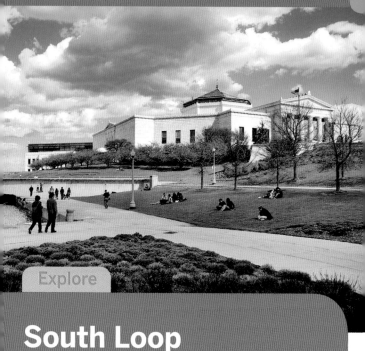

Explore

South Loop & Near South Side

In the South Loop, the Field Museum, Shedd Aquarium and Adler Planetarium huddle at the Museum Campus. Peaceful 12th Street Beach and hilly Northerly Island offer nearby refuges to ditch the crowds. Historic buildings dot the neighborhood, including Chess Records, the seminal blues label. Chinatown bustles with noodle shops and exotic wares.

The Sights in a Day

☀ Spend the morning at the Museum Campus, and take your pick of sights. The **Field Museum of Natural History** (p114) offers dinosaurs, mummies and gemstones. **Adler Planetarium** (p118) has telescopes and starry films.

☀ Stay at the Museum Campus and explore nearby **Northerly Island** (p118) and **12th Street Beach** (p119). **Lou Malnati's** (p120) makes a fine refueling stop, or head to **Qing Xiang Yuan Dumplings** (p120) in Chinatown. Blues diehards should make the pilgrimage to **Willie Dixon's Blues Heaven** (p119). The beer garden at **Spoke & Bird** (p122) is a splendid way to blow the rest of the afternoon.

☾ If it's Friday, Saturday or Sunday, put on your dancing shoes and groove to world beats at **SummerDance** (p118). Share tapas for dinner at convivial **Mercat a la Planxa** (p120). See who's bending frets at **Buddy Guy's Legends** (p122), the iconic bluesman's club and the city's best for the genre. If jazz is your sound, head to **Jazz Showcase** (p123) for a top-tier show.

Top Sight

 Field Museum of Natural History (p114)

♥ Best of Chicago

Museums & Galleries

Field Museum of Natural History (p114)

Museum of Contemporary Photography (p118)

Adler Planetarium (p118)

Live Music

Buddy Guy's Legends (p122)

Jazz Showcase (p123)

Parks & Gardens

Northerly Island (p118)

Comedy & Performing Arts

SummerDance (p118)

For Kids

12th Street Beach (p119)

Getting There

🚌 **Bus** Numbers 130 (in summer) and 146 (year-round) go to the Museum Campus. Bus 1 runs along Michigan Ave.

Ⓜ **El** Red Line to Harrison and Red, Orange, Green Line to Roosevelt for South Loop. Red Line to Cermak-Chinatown for Chinatown.

Top Sights
Field Museum of Natural History

The mammoth Field Museum of Natural History houses everything but the kitchen sink. The collection's rock star is Sue, the largest *Tyrannosaurus rex* yet discovered. She's 13ft tall and 41ft long, and menaces the main floor with ferocious aplomb. The galleries beyond hold 30 million other artifacts, tended by a slew of PhD-wielding scientists, as the Field remains an active research institution.

👁 Map p116, C4

☎ 312-922-9410

www.fieldmuseum.org

1400 S Lake Shore Dr

adult/child $22/15

🕘 9am-5pm

🚌 146, 130

Dinosaur skeleton model, Field Museum of Natural History

Dinosaur Stash

After communing with Sue, dino lovers should head up to the 'Evolving Planet' exhibit on the 2nd floor, which has more of the big guys and gals. You can learn about the evolution of various species and watch staff paleontologists clean up fossils in the lab. Don't miss the exhibit where you try to pull yourself out of the Ice Age tar pit.

Mummies Galore

'Inside Ancient Egypt' is another good exhibit that re-creates an Egyptian burial chamber on two levels. The mastaba (tomb) contains 23 actual mummies and is a reconstruction of the one built for Unis-ankh, the son of the last pharaoh of the Fifth dynasty, who died at age 21 in 2407 BC. The relic-strewn bottom level is especially worthwhile.

Gems & Stuffed Animals

Other displays that merit your time include the Hall of Gems and its glittering garnets, opals, emeralds, pearls and diamonds. The Northwest Coast and Arctic Peoples' totem-pole collection got its start with artifacts shipped to Chicago for the 1893 World's Expo. And the largest man-eating lion ever caught is stuffed and standing sentry on the basement floor. Preserved insects and birds, and Bushman, the cantankerous ape who drew crowds at Lincoln Park Zoo for decades, are also on display in all their taxidermic glory.

☑ Top Tips

▸ Ask for the 'Basic' admission to see everything mentioned here.

▸ The 'All Access' and 'Discovery' admission tickets include extras such as the 3-D movie and special exhibits, which can be too much if you're doing lots of sightseeing.

▸ The museum is vast, so get a map at the desk and make a plan of attack to see your top choices.

▸ The various shops inside are worth a browse for their abundant dino gear and educational toys.

▸ Download the museum's free app for curated tours of various collections.

✗ Take a Break

Relax in the beer garden and chomp into tavern-style pizza at Flo & Santos (p122). Fuel up on crepes, French toast and omelets at bright and cheery Yolk (p120) – worth the potentially long wait.

Lake Michigan

Ferry to Near Navy

Shedd
Aquarium
◉ 3

Adler ◉ 4
Planetarium

Charter One

E Solidarity Dr

Lakefront Trail

S Lake Shore Dr

MUSEUM
CAMPUS

Field
Museum of
Natural History
◉

E McFetridge Dr

Museum Campus /
11th St (Metra)
Ⓐ

41

S Lake Shore

Grant Park

Hutchinson
Field

E Balbo Ave

E Congress Pkwy

Grant
Park

Tennis
Courts

Grant
Park

E Roosevelt Rd

S Indiana Ave

Webster
Park

S Columbus Dr

Museum of
Contemporary
Photography
◉ 1

Spiritof
Music Garden

✖ 7

E Harrison St

E 8th St

E 9th St

E 11th St

S Michigan S

Roosevelt

Ⓜ

✖ 10

CENTRAL
STATION

E 13th St

✖ 11

E 14th St

Grant
Park

E Van Buren St

S State St

W Van Buren St

E Congress Pkwy

S Clark St

W Harrison St

S Plymouth Ct

S Dearborn St

Harrison
Ⓜ

S State St

❶ 14

◉ 16

SOUTH
LOOP

S Holden Ct

✖ 9

❸ 15

W Polk St

S Federal St

S 9th St

DEARBORN
PARK

W Roosevelt Rd

Jones
Park

Plymouth Ct

S State St

S Clark St

S State St

Lake
Michigan

500 m
0.25 miles

Ⓝ

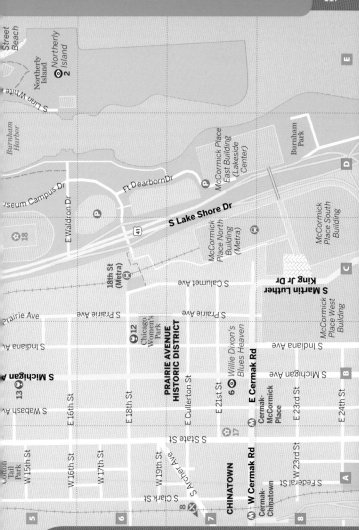

Sights

Museum of Contemporary Photography
MUSEUM

1 ⊙ Map p116, B2

This small museum focuses on American and international photography from the early 20th century onward, and is the only institution of its kind between the coasts. The permanent collection includes the works of Henri Cartier-Bresson, Harry Callahan, Sally Mann, Victor Skrebneski, Catherine Wagner and 500 more of the best photographers working today. Special exhibitions (also free) augment the rotating permanent collection. (☑312-663-5554; www.mocp. org; 600 S Michigan Ave, Columbia College; admission free; ⊙10am-5pm Mon-Wed, Fri & Sat, to 8pm Thu, noon-5pm Sun; M Red Line to Harrison)

Local Life
SummerDance

To boogie with a multi-ethnic mash-up of locals, head to the Spirit of Music Garden in Grant Park for **SummerDance** (Map p116, B2; www. chicagosummerdance.org; 601 S Michigan Ave; ⊙6-9:30pm Fri & Sat, 4-7pm Sun late Jun-mid-Sep; M Red Line to Harrison). Bands play rumba, samba and other world beats preceded by fun dance lessons – all free. Ballroom-quality moves are absolutely not required.

Northerly Island
PARK

2 ⊙ Map p116, E5

This hilly, prairie-grassed park has a walking and cycling trail, fishing, bird-watching and an outdoor venue for big-name concerts. It's actually a peninsula, not an island, but the Chicago skyline views are tremendous no matter what you call it. Stop in at the field house, if it's open, for tour information. Bicycles are available at the Divvy bike-share station by the Adler Planetarium. Note that parts of the trail are closed at times due to weather damage. (1521 S Linn White Dr; 🚊146, 130)

Shedd Aquarium
AQUARIUM

3 ⊙ Map p116, D3

Top draws at the kiddie-mobbed Shedd Aquarium include the Wild Reef exhibit, where there's just 5in of Plexiglas between you and two-dozen fierce-looking sharks, and the Oceanarium, with its rescued sea otters. Note the Oceanarium also keeps beluga whales and Pacific white-sided dolphins, a practice that has become increasingly controversial in recent years. (☑312-939-2438; www.sheddaquarium.org; 1200 S Lake Shore Dr; adult/child $40/30; ⊙9am-6pm Jun-Aug, 9am-5pm Mon-Fri, to 6pm Sat & Sun Sep-May; 🚼; 🚊146, 130)

Adler Planetarium
MUSEUM

4 ⊙ Map p116, E4

Space enthusiasts will get a big bang (pun!) out of the Adler. There are public telescopes to view the stars (10am to

Adler Planetarium

1pm daily, by the Galileo Cafe), 3-D lectures to learn about supernovas (in the Space Visualization Lab), and the Planet Explorers exhibit where kids can 'launch' a rocket. The immersive digital films cost extra (from $13 per ticket). The Adler's front steps offer Chicago's best skyline view, so get your camera ready. (☏ 312-922-7827; www.adlerplanetarium.org; 1300 S Lake Shore Dr; adult/child $12/8; ☺ 9:30am-4pm; ⛟; 🚌 146, 130)

12th Street Beach   BEACH

5 ◎ Map p116, E5

A path runs south from the Adler Planetarium to this crescent of sand. Despite its proximity to the visitor-mobbed Museum Campus, the small beach remains bizarrely (but happily) secluded. Bonus: if you can't get tickets to see your favorite band at the Pavilion at Northerly Island, you can sit here and still hear the tunes. (www.cpdbeaches.com; 1200 S Linn White Dr; 🚌 146, 130)

Willie Dixon's
Blues Heaven   HISTORIC BUILDING

6 ◎ Map p116, B7

From 1957 to 1967, this humble building was Chess Records, the seminal electric blues label. It's now named for the bassist who wrote most of Chess' hits. Staff give hour-long tours of the premises. It's pretty ramshackle, with few original artifacts on display. Still, when Willie's grandson hauls out the bluesman's well-worn stand-up bass and lets you take a pluck, it's pretty cool. Call first; opening times can be erratic. (📞 312-808-1286; www.bluesheaven.com; 2120 S Michigan Ave; tours $10; ⏱ by appointment Wed & Thu, noon-4pm Fri, to 3pm Sat; Ⓜ Green Line to Cermak-McCormick Pl)

Eating

Mercat a la Planxa   SPANISH $$$

7 ✖️ Map p116, B2

This Barcelona-style tapas and seafood restaurant buzzes in an enormous, convivial room where light streams in through the floor-to-ceiling windows. It cooks all the specialties of Catalonia and stokes a festive atmosphere, enhanced by copious quantities of *cava* (sparkling wine) and sangria. It's located in the beaux-arts **Blackstone Hotel** (Map p116, B2; 📞 312-447-0524; www. blackstonerenaissance.com; r $199-319; 🅿 ❄ @ 🛜 ♿). (📞 312-765-0524; www. mercatchicago.com; 638 S Michigan Ave; tapas $10-17, tasting menus from $65; ⏱ 11am-10pm Mon-Thu, to 11pm Fri, 10am-11pm Sat, 10am-10pm Sun; Ⓜ Red Line to Harrison)

Qing Xiang Yuan Dumplings   DUMPLINGS $

8 ✖️ Map p116, A7

The name doesn't lie: it's all about dumplings in this bright room under bamboo lanterns. They come steamed by the dozen, with fillings such as lamb and coriander, ground pork and cabbage, sea whelk and leek, and some 30 other types. Bite into one and a hot

shot of flavor erupts in your mouth. Located upstairs in the Richland Center food court. (📞 312-799-1118; www. qxydumplings.com; 2002 S Wentworth Ave, Ste 103; mains $8-12; ⏱ 11am-11pm; Ⓜ Red Line to Cermak-Chinatown)

Lou Malnati's   PIZZA $

9 ✖️ Map p116, A2

Lou Malnati's is one of the city's premier deep-dish pizza makers. In fact, it claims to have invented the gooey behemoth (though that's a matter of never-ending dispute). Not in dispute: the deliciousness of Malnati's famed butter crust. Gluten-free diners can opt for the sausage crust (it's literally just meat, no dough). The restaurant has outlets citywide. (📞 312-786-1000; www. loumalnatis.com; 805 S State St; small pizzas from $13; ⏱ 11am-11pm Sun-Thu, to midnight Fri & Sat; Ⓜ Red Line to Harrison)

Yolk   BREAKFAST $

10 ✖️ Map p116, B3

This cheerful diner is worth the long wait – you'll dig into the best traditional breakfast in the South Loop. The omelets include lots of healthy options (the Iron Man is made from egg whites and comes loaded with veggies and avocado), and sweets lovers have stacks of cinnamon-roll French toast and peach-cobbler crepes to drench in syrup. (📞 312-789-9655; www.eatyolk.com; 1120 S Michigan Ave; mains $10-14; ⏱ 6am-3pm Mon-Fri, 7am-3pm Sat & Sun; ♿; Ⓜ Red, Orange, Green Line to Roosevelt)

Understand

Sounds of Chicago

Blues

Chicago's most famous musical style comes in one color: blue. After the Great Migration of African Americans out of the rural South, Delta blues-men set up on Chicago's street corners and in the open-air markets of Maxwell St during the 1930s. That's when Robert Johnson first recorded 'Sweet Home Chicago.' What distinguishes Chicago's regional blues style from Johnson's original ode is simple: volume. Chicago blues is defined by electric guitars plugged in to amplifiers. Muddy Waters and Howlin' Wolf were the first to create the new sound. Bluesmen from the 1950s and '60s, such as Willie Dixon, Junior Wells and Elmore James, and later champions like Buddy Guy, Koko Taylor and Otis Rush, became national stars of the genre.

House

Chicago's other big taste-making musical export took root in the early '80s at a now-defunct West Loop nightclub called the Warehouse. The venue's DJ, Frankie Knuckles, got tired of spinning disco and added samples of European electronic music and beats from that new-fangled invention, the stand-alone drum machine. And so house music was born (named after Knuckles' club). Uninterested in appeal-ing to commercial radio, the tracks used deep, pounding bass beats and instrumental samples made for dancing. House music DJs such as Derrick Carter and Larry Heard revolutionized the form and huge second-wave stars like Felix da Housecat, DJ Sneak and acid-house artist Armando took Chicago's thump worldwide.

Jazz & Rock

The Great Migration also helped the city become a jazz hotbed, especially in the 1920s. Louis Armstrong and Earl 'Fatha' Hines were part of the house band at the famed Sunset Cafe in Bronzeville (now defunct). Chicago still fosters an active, avant-garde scene. In recent decades the underground rock community has filled an important niche. Local record labels such as Touch and Go, Bloodshot and Thrill Jockey popped up in the 1980s and '90s, and the city became a hub for post-rock, alt country and noise rock bands. The reigning kings of Chicago rock are (arguably) still Wilco.

Flo & Santos PUB FOOD $$

11 Map p116, B4

This pub is known for its tavern-style pizza (with wafer-thin crust and sweet sauce) and its Polish dishes (like pierogi and potato pancakes). Eat in the warm, exposed-brick interior or in the outdoor beer garden at umbrella-shaded picnic tables under strands of winking lights. (📞312-566-9817; www.floandsantos.com; 1310 S Wabash Ave; mains $12-19; ⏰11:30am-11pm Sun-Thu, to midnight Fri & Sat; Ⓜ Red, Orange, Green Line to Roosevelt)

Drinking

Spoke & Bird CAFE

12 Map p116, B6

The South Loop has been begging for a leafy patio like the one at Spoke & Bird. Bonus: it's surrounded by several cool old manors in the Prairie Avenue Historic District. Relax with a locally made brew and nifty cafe fare such as the sweet parsnip muffin or lamb barbecue

 Top Tip
Free Blues Concerts
Buddy Guy's Legends hosts free, all-ages acoustic performances from noon to 2pm Wednesday through Sunday. Listen in while having lunch (it's also a Cajun restaurant) or a drink at the bar. Free blues concerts also rock the side garden at Willie Dixon's Blues Heaven (p119) on Thursdays at 6pm in summer.

sandwich. (www.spokeandbird.com; 205 E 18th St; ⏰7am-6pm; 🛜; 🚆1)

Vice District Brewing MICROBREWERY

13 Map p116, B5

Vice is a favorite gathering spot for South Loop residents. The large, mod-industrial taproom is just right for a pint of black IPA or English-style bitter ale. Many drinkers stop in pre-Bears game. It's not far from Soldier Field, and it opens early (11am) on Sunday game days. (📞312-291-9022; www.vicedis trictbrewing.com; 1454 S Michigan Ave; ⏰4-11pm Tue-Thu, to 1am Fri, 2pm-1am Sat, to 9pm Sun; Ⓜ Green, Orange, Red Line to Roosevelt)

Kasey's Tavern PUB

14 Map p116, A2

Kasey's is a friendly neighborhood pub that draws a mix of artsy students from the nearby universities, local condo dwellers and sports fans, all of whom sit at the wooden bar. There's something for everyone on the enormous beer list. Scads of flat-screen TVs show Chicago's teams in action. (📞312-427-7992; www.kaseystavern.com; 701 S Dearborn St; ⏰11am-2am; Ⓜ Red Line to Harrison)

Entertainment

Buddy Guy's Legends BLUES

15 ⭐ Map p116, B2

Top local and national acts wail on the stage of local icon Buddy Guy.

The man himself usually plugs in his axe for a series of shows in January (tickets go on sale in November). The location is a bit rough around the edges, but the acts are consistently excellent. (☎312-427-1190; www.buddyguy. com; 700 S Wabash Ave; tickets Sun-Thu $10, Fri & Sat $20; ⏱5pm-2am Mon & Tue, from 11am Wed-Fri, noon-3am Sat, to 2am Sun; Ⓜ Red Line to Harrison)

Buddy Guy performing at Buddy Guy's Legends

Jazz Showcase   JAZZ

 16 ⭐ Map p116, A2

The Jazz Showcase, set in a gorgeous room in historic Dearborn Station, is Chicago's top club for national names. In general, local musicians take the stage Monday through Wednesday, with visiting jazz cats blowing their horns Thursday through Sunday. (☎312-360-0234; www.jazzshowcase.com; 806 S Plymouth Ct; tickets $20-35; Ⓜ Red Line to Harrison)

Reggies   LIVE MUSIC

17 ⭐ Map p116, A7

Bring on the punk and the all-ages shows. Graffitied Reggies books mostly touring hard-core bands at the Rock Club. Next door, Reggies' Music Joint is for folks 21 and older, and hosts more mainstream (we use that term loosely) live music nightly. Reggies also provides shuttle buses to various Bears and White Sox games and other events. (☎312-949-0121; www.reggieslive.com; 2109 S State St; ⏱11am-2am; Ⓜ Green Line to Cermak-McCormick Pl)

Chicago Bears   FOOTBALL

18 ⭐ Map p116, C5

Da Bears, Chicago's NFL team, tackle at **Soldier Field** (Map p116, C5; ☎312-235-7152; www.soldierfield.net; 1410 S Museum Campus Dr; tours adult/child $15/4; 🚌146, 130) from September through January. Arrive early on game days and wander through the parking lots – you won't believe the elaborate tailgate feasts people cook up from the back of their cars. And seriously, dress warmly. If you can't score a ticket, hit one of the South Loop bars to watch the game. (☎847-615-2327; www.chicagobears.com; 1410 S Museum Campus Dr; 🚌146, 128)

PAUL NATKIN/GETTY IMAGES ©

Local Life
A Bookish Day in Hyde Park

Getting There

🚌 Bus 10 from Michigan Ave to MSI during museum hours; otherwise bus 6 from State St.

🚆 Electric Line from Loop's Millennium Station to 51st-53rd or 55th-56th-57th stops.

The University of Chicago and its grand Gothic buildings dominate Hyde Park. Faculty and students have racked up more than 80 Nobel Prizes within those hallowed halls. It's no surprise, then, that a ramble here involves brainy bookstores and make-you-think museums, with the neighborhood's favorite dive bar and soul-food cafe thrown in for good measure.

1 57th Street Beach

Just across Lake Shore Dr from the Museum of Science & Industry, **57th Street Beach** (www.cpdbeaches.com; 5700 S Lake Shore Dr) is a mellow stretch of sand where neighborhood families and college kids come to hit the waves. Surfers say it's the best beach to hang ten.

2 Museum of Science & Industry

Geek out at the **Museum of Science & Industry** (MSI; ☎773-684-1414; www.msichicago.org; 5700 S Lake Shore Dr; adult/child $18/11; ⏱9:30am-5:30pm Jun-Aug, shorter hours Sep-May; ♿), the western hemisphere's largest science collection. Highlights include a WWII German U-boat ($12 extra to tour) and the 'Science Storms' mock tornado.

3 Powell's

Used bookstore **Powell's** (☎773-955-7780; www.powellschicago.com; 1501 E 57th St; ⏱9am-11pm) can get you just about any title ever published. Shelf after heaving shelf props up the well-arranged stock. Staff often put a box of tattered free books outside by the entrance.

4 Robie House

Of the numerous buildings that Frank Lloyd Wright designed around Chicago, none is more famous or influential than **Robie House** (☎312-994-4000; www.flwright.org; 5757 S Woodlawn Ave; adult/child $18/15; ⏱10:30am-3pm Thu-Mon), his horizontal-lined, Prairie-style masterwork. Inside are 174 stained-glass windows and doors, which you'll see on the tours (frequency varies by season).

5 Seminary Co-op Bookstore

At academic **Seminary Co-op Bookstore** (☎773-752-4381; www.semcoop.com; 5751 S Woodlawn Ave; ⏱8:30am-8pm Mon-Fri, 10am-6pm Sat, noon-6pm Sun), you might run into a Nobel laureate or three. Local scholars adore this place, where you'll find no fewer than eight versions of *War and Peace* on the shelves.

6 Jimmy's Woodlawn Tap

Jimmy's Woodlawn Tap (☎773-643-5516; 1172 E 55th St; ⏱10:30am-2am Mon-Fri, from 11am Sat & Sun) is dark and beery, and a little seedy. But for thousands of University of Chicago students deprived of a thriving bar scene, it's home. Hungry? The Swiss burgers are legendary.

7 Valois Cafeteria

The neighborhood clientele at **Valois** (☎773-667-0647; www.valoisrestaurant.com; 1518 E 53rd St; mains $6-14; ⏱5:30am-10pm) is so socioeconomically diverse that a U of C sociology professor wrote a book about it, titled *Slim's Table*. It seems Southern-style catfish, biscuits and pot pies attract all kinds – even Barack Obama, who chowed here regularly when he lived nearby.

8 Promontory

The **Promontory** (☎312-801-2100; www.promontorychicago.com; 5311 S Lake Park Ave) is Hyde Park's first hipster music hall. The rustic, huge-window room hosts jazz, soul and funk musicians, as well as DJs several nights a week. Even if there's no show, you can have a glass of wine at the bar and munch a wood-oven-roasted veggie sandwich.

The Best of
Chicago

Chicago's Best Walks

Chicago's Best...

Pritzker Pavilion (p25), Millennium Park
F11PHOTO/SHUTTERSTOCK ©

Best Walks
Skyscrapers & Street Art

🏃 The Walk

It's hard to know what to gawk at first. High-flying architecture is everywhere, thanks to Mrs O'Leary's cow (who allegedly kicked over the lantern that burned down the city in 1871, and created the blank canvas for lofty new designs). Whimsical public art adds to the eye-candy. This tour swoops through the Loop, taking in the best of it all, from sky-high record breakers to art-deco landmarks, a pink flamingo and the shiny Bean, plus a visit to Al Capone's dentist thrown in for good measure.

Start Daley Plaza; Blue Line to Washington

Finish Willis Tower; Brown, Orange, Purple, Pink Line to Quincy

Length 1.25 miles; one hour

🍴 Take a Break

Fortify with a Scotch egg and glass of whiskey at the buzzy **Gage** (p36).

FELIX LIPOV/SHUTTERSTOCK ©

Board of Trade building

❶ Picasso's Untitled

Picasso's abstract **Untitled** (p34) sculpture is ensconced in Daley Plaza. He never would say what the 1967 iron work represents. Most people believe it's the head of a woman. But Picasso also drew pictures of his dog that look similar. Go ahead and climb on it.

❷ Reliance Building

Head to the corner of Washington and State Sts and check out the shimmering 1890s Reliance Building. Its lightweight frame made it the precedent for the modern skyscraper. Today it houses the chic **Alise Chicago** hotel. Added historical bonus: Al Capone's dentist drilled teeth in what's now Room 809.

❸ Chicago Cultural Center

The 1897 **Chicago Cultural Center** (p34) is a beaux-arts beauty in its own right, but you're here to get inspiration from the architectural photos in the 1st-floor Landmark Gallery. The exhibit shows 72 images of prominent structures, several that have since been demolished.

④ The Bean

Enter Millennium Park and view the silvery sculpture everyone calls 'the Bean.' Artist Anish Kapoor officially titled it **Cloud Gate** (p25) but no matter. Join the masses swarming it to see the skyline's reflection.

⑤ Art Institute of Chicago

The **Art Institute** (p28) is one of Chicago's most-visited attractions, and the 1894 bronze lions out front are city mascots of sorts. They remain regal and dignified even when the museum plops fiberglass Blackhawks helmets on their heads during Stanley Cup wins.

⑥ Flamingo

Alexander Calder's **Flamingo** gives a bit of color and contrast to famed architect Ludwig Mies van der Rohe's blocky, black Kluczynski Building behind it. The 'bird' is made of 50 tons of bright red steel.

⑦ Chicago Board of Trade

The **Board of Trade** is a 1930 art-deco gem. It stands as a gateway to Chicago's financial district. A giant state of Ceres, the goddess of agriculture, tops the 45-story edifice.

⑧ Willis Tower

The **Willis Tower** (p30) is Chicago's tallest skyscraper at 1450ft. Ascend to the 103rd-floor Skydeck to look over the high-rises and artworks you've just traversed.

Best Walks
Mansions, Beaches & Greenery

🏃 The Walk

The Gold Coast and Lincoln Park are among Chicago's most prized bits of real estate, but they didn't start that way. The former was a swamp, the latter a cemetery c1865. That changed when Lake Shore Dr opened, and Bertha and Potter Palmer built a manor at its edge. So began a rush of Chicago's wealthy to the neighborhood. The park became their fashionable playground (the cemetery was moved). This walk explores the area's past and present.

Start Original Playboy Mansion; Red Line to Clark/Division

Finish Caldwell Lily Pool; bus 151

Length 3 miles; 2½ hours

🍴 Take a Break

The **Patio at Cafe Brauer** (2021 N Stockton Dr; mains $9-13; ⏰11am-9pm Mon-Fri, from 8:30am Sat & Sun; 🚼) is perfect for a glass of wine while sitting by the zoo's South Pond.

Astor Street (p65)

STEVGGER/GETTY IMAGES ©

❶ Original Playboy Mansion

Hugh Hefner began wearing his all-day jammies at this 1927 **mansion** (p62), when the rigors of magazine production and partying prevented him from getting dressed. The building contains condos now, so you can't enter, but you can let your imagination run wild about the parties Hef had.

❷ Astor Street

Head east to **Astor St** (p65). It was named for John Jacob Astor, one of the USA's richest citizens when he died in 1848. Astor never lived here, but the area's builders thought his name added dazzle. Several turn-of-the-century mansions rise up between the 1300 and 1500 blocks.

❸ Charnley-Persky House

While he was still working for famed architect Louis Sullivan, Frank Lloyd Wright (who was 19 at the time) designed the **Charnley-Persky House**. It was completed in 1892 and now houses the Society of Architectural Historians.

4 North Avenue Beach

Head northeast through the park (past the bikeshare, then toward the underpass) to **North Avenue Beach** (p72). It's Chicago's most popular sand lot. A short walk on the breakwater yields postcard skyline views.

5 Nature Boardwalk

From the beach, walk over the pedestrian bridge back into Lincoln Park. Amble around the **Nature Boardwalk**, a half-mile path around the South Pond's wetlands ecosystem.

6 Lincoln Park Zoo

Mosey northward through the free **zoo** (p72), which has been entertaining locals for around 150 years. Zebras, snow monkeys and rhinos are among the critters that flash quickly by.

7 Lincoln Park Conservatory

Continue north to the **conservatory** (p73). The fine 1891 hothouse coaxes ferns, orchids and palms to flourish. In winter, it becomes an escape from the icy winds raging outside.

8 Caldwell Lily Pool

The enchanting **Caldwell Lily Pool** (p69) hides in a plot northeast of the conservatory. It's a lovely escape from the crowd, with Prairie-style stonework, lazing turtles and dragonflies fluttering around.

Best
Architecture

The Great Fire of 1871 sparked an architectural revolution in Chicago. It created a blank slate where new ideas could be tested. Daniel Burnham, one of the prime designers during the era, encouraged architects to think big and not be put off by traditional limits. Chicago has been a hotbed for skyscraper design ever since.

Architects to Know

You'll hear these names often as you explore the city. Louis Sullivan was Chicago's architectural founding father, a revolutionary of steel-frame high-rises. Frank Lloyd Wright was Sullivan's student, who catapulted the Prairie style to global renown. Daniel Burnham was the man with the plan that preserved Chicago's lakefront. Ludwig Mies van der Rohe was known for his 'less is more' motto and simple, boxy designs for modern skyscrapers. Jeanne Gang is the city's current starchitect. Her mod, organic structures are popping up all over the city.

Preservation

The Chicago Architecture Foundation – known today for its great tours and gift shop – grew out of a 1960s preservation effort to save a South Loop home. The group was successful with that building, but many others met the wrecking ball. The most famous was the Stock Exchange Building, designed by Louis Sullivan and Dankmar Adler. You can still see a bit of it, as the Stock Exchange Arch was salvaged and now stands outside the Art Institute (on the northeast side). Several groups have since sprung up to ensure Chicago's worthy buildings live on.

☑ Top Tips

▶ For DIY explorations of Chicago's steely structures, staff at the Chicago Architecture Foundation recommend using the *Pocket Guide to Chicago Architecture* by Judith Paine McBrien or *A View from the River*, the foundation's book that highlights buildings along its popular tour-boat routes.

▶ The local public TV station offers a great, free mobile guide and audio tour of downtown architecture. It's available at http://interactive. wttw.com/loop.

Best Skyscrapers

Willis Tower Ascend 103 floors in Chicago's tallest building, then peer down from a glass-floored ledge. (p30)

360° Chicago Get high at the John Hancock tower's 94th-floor observatory or 96th-floor lounge. (p56)

Tribune Tower This neo-Gothic cloud-poker is in-laid with stones from the Taj Mahal, the Parthenon and more. (p48)

Marina City The groovy corn-cob towers look like something from a *Jetsons* cartoon. (p48; pictured left)

Water Tower The only downtown survivor of the 1871 Great Fire was a skyscraper in its day. (p62)

Best Prairie Style

Robie House The low eves and graceful lines of Frank Lloyd Wright's masterpiece were emulated around the world. (p125)

Rookery Wright gave the atrium a light-filled renovation that features 'floating' staircases. (p35)

Best Beaux Arts

Chicago Cultural Center Gilded ceilings, rich marble walls and mother-of-pearl mosaics bejewel the halls. (p34)

Museum of Science & Industry It was the classical Palace of Fine Arts at the landmark 1893 World's Expo. (p125)

Best Mansions

Driehaus Museum A Gilded Age manor with three floors of gorgeous decorative arts and stained glass. (p48)

Original Playboy Mansion Hugh Hefner and the Playboy bunnies used to swing in this Gold Coast beauty. (p62)

Cyrus McCormick Mansion A turn-of-the-century neoclassical home that's a relic from when Astor St was millionaires' row. (p65)

 Worth a Trip

Frank Lloyd Wright Home & Studio (☎312-994-4000; www.flwright.org; 951 Chicago Ave; adult/child $18/15; ◷10am-4pm), in suburban Oak Park, offers a fascinating, hour-long walk-through of the famed architect's abode from 1889 to 1909. It's easy to reach via the Green Line train from downtown Chicago.

Best
Eating

Chicago has become a chowhound's hot spot. For the most part, restaurants here are reasonably priced and pretension-free, serving masterful food in come-as-you-are environs. You can also fork into a superb range of ethnic eats, especially if you break out of downtown and head for neighborhoods such as Pilsen or Uptown.

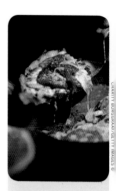

CHARITY BURGGRAAF/GETTY IMAGES ©

Local Specialties

Foremost is deep-dish pizza (pictured above right), with crust that rises two or three inches above the plate and cradles a molten pile of toppings. One gooey piece is practically a meal. No less iconic is the Chicago hot dog – a wiener in a poppy-seed bun with a litany of toppings (including onions, tomatoes, a dill pickle and neon-green relish, but never ketchup). The city is also revered for its spicy, drippy, only-in-Chicago Italian beef sandwiches.

Eat Streets

Chicago's best and brightest chefs cook on Randolph St in the West Loop. Copious sidewalk seating spills out of hip bistros and cafes on Division St in Wicker Park. Mexican taquerias mix meet hipster hangouts along 18th St in Pilsen.

Chefs to Know

Rick Bayless is everywhere: on TV, tending the organic garden where he grows his restaurants' herbs, and operating Xoco (p50) among his various eateries. Grant Achatz made 'molecular gastronomy' a culinary catchphrase at Alinea (p74); his other hot spots include Roister (p106). Stephanie Izard gained fame for winning *Top Chef* and *Iron Chef Gauntlet*. She now runs Girl & the Goat (p107), Little Goat (p106) and more.

☑ Top Tips

▸ Make dinner reservations for eateries in the midrange and upper price brackets, especially on weekends.

▸ Many restaurants let you book online through OpenTable (www.opentable.com).

▸ Need help deciding where to eat? LTH Forum (www.lthforum.com) is a great local resource.

Best for Chowhounds

Alinea Molecular gastronomy at one of the world's best restaurants. (p74)

Longman & Eagle Michelin-starred, shabby-chic tavern for breakfast, lunch or dinner. (p99)

Girl & the Goat Rockin' ambience and dishes starring the titular animal. (p107)

Revival Food Hall A slew of all-local, hipster eats to choose from. (p37)

Best Budget

Pleasant House Pub Savory pies and fish fries. (p109)

Irazu Chicago's lone Costa Rican eatery whips up distinctive, peppery fare. (p93)

Xoco Celeb chef Rick Bayless' Mexican street-food hut. (p50)

Publican Quality Meats Beefy sandwiches straight from the butcher's block. (p103)

Best Neighborhood Gems

Hopleaf Locals pile in for the mussels, *frites* and 200-strong beer list. (p87)

Dove's Luncheonette Sit at the retro counter for Tex-Mex dishes, pie and whiskey. (p92)

Ruxbin Teeny spot where passionate chefs cook artful dinners. (p92)

mfk Romantic hole-in-the-wall for unfussy Spanish seafood. (p83)

Best Pizza

Giordano's It's like deep-dish on steroids, with awesomely bulked-up crusts. (p50)

Pequod's Pizza Sweet sauce and caramelized cheese. (p74)

Pizano's Makes a great thin crust to supplement the deep dish. (p37)

Best Hot Dogs

Hot G Dog Goes beyond gourmet weenies, with a killer Chicago-style dog too. (p87)

Wieners Circle Char-dogs, cheddar fries and lots of unruly swearing. (p75)

Best Brunch

Big Jones Dishes from New Orleans and the Carolina Lowcountry. (p87)

Flo Hungover hipsters crave the breakfast burritos. (p94)

Best Vegetarian

Mana Food Bar Swanky all-veg eatery that makes dishes from around the globe. (p93)

Handlebar Bike messenger hangout with many meat-free dishes on the menu. (p94)

Native Foods Cafe Loop outpost of the national chain of vegan fast-casual restaurants. (p37)

Best Sweets

Hendrickx Belgian Bread Crafter Buttery waffles and dark chocolate croissants. (p64)

Doughnut Vault Enormous, pillowy doughnuts sold from a teeny, tiny shop. (p50)

Best
Museums & Galleries

The world's largest Tyrannosaurus rex? The most impressionist paintings outside of France? The western hemisphere's biggest science museum? These are all superlatives that belong to Chicago's institutions, which draw millions of visitors each year. If big museums aren't your thing, the city has a fine assortment of smaller venues covering everything from Mexican beadwork to antique amputation saws, plus galleries galore.

Online Tickets

Most major museums allow you to buy tickets online. The advantage is that you're assured entry and; at many venues, you get to skip the regular ticket lines. The disadvantage is that sometimes you have to pay a service fee ($2 or so), and at times the prepay line is almost as long as the regular one. Our suggestion: consider buying online in summer and for big exhibits. Otherwise, there's no need.

Gallery Districts

Chicago has five gallery-rich zones. River North is the most entrenched, where top international names show off their works; it also has the largest concentration of galleries. The West Loop is a hotbed of edgy, avant-garde art that garners international praise. Bucktown and Wicker Park are rife with alternative spaces and emerging talent. Pilsen hosts several small, artist-run spaces that have erratic hours. And the South Side neighborhood of Bridgeport has become a player with cool-cat galleries in a warren of old warehouses on W 35th St.

NAEBLYS/SHUTTERSTOCK ©

☑ Top Tips

▶ The Go Chicago Card (www.smartdestinations.com/chicago) allows you to visit an unlimited number of attractions for a flat fee. It's good for one, two, three or five consecutive days.

▶ The company also offers a three-, four- or five-choice 'Explorer Pass'; where you pick among 25 options for sights. It's valid for 30 days.

Best Art Museums

Art Institute of Chicago
Gawk at Monets, modern works, miniatures and more at the nation's second-largest art museum. (p28)

Museum of Contemporary Art Consider it the Art Institute's unruly sibling: a collection that always pushes boundaries. (p58)

National Museum of Mexican Art It holds a terrific collection of paintings, altars, folk art and politically charged pieces. (p106)

Best Science Museums

Field Museum of Natural History Explore collections of dinosaurs, gems, mummies and taxidermied lions. (p114)

Museum of Science & Industry You could spend an entire day in the western hemisphere's largest science museum. (p125)

Adler Planetarium Journey to the nether regions of outer space at this lakeside gem. (p118; pictured above left)

Best Galleries

Intuit: the Center for Intuitive & Outsider Art
Holds a museum-quality display of folk art. (p92)

Mars Gallery It's pop art presided over by a kitty cat (he's the assistant manager). (p102)

Galerie F One-of-a-kind, rock and roll gallery for gig posters and street art. (p99)

Best Offbeat Museums

Money Museum You'll emerge richer than when you entered, thanks to a take-home bag of shredded currency. (p35)

International Museum of Surgical Science Amputation saws, iron lungs and a roomful of cadaver murals cram a creepy old mansion. (p62)

Best Underappreciated Museums

Chicago History Museum Tells the city's story with artifacts such as Prohibition-era booze stills. (p72)

Museum of Contemporary Photography Tidy and engaging (and free), it's a great stop in the South Loop. (p118)

Peggy Notebaert Nature Museum Hands-on, family-oriented spot with a turtle-filled marsh and butterfly garden. (p73)

Depaul Art Museum The university's free venue hosts engaging exhibits of 20th century works. (p74)

Worth a Trip

Bridgeport has become a pocket of artsy cool. Side-by-side **Zhou B Art Center** (☏773-523-0200; www.zhoubart-center.com; 1029 W 35th St; ⊙main exhibition spaces 10am-5pm Mon-Sat; 🚌8) and **Bridgeport Art Center** (☏773-247-3000; www.bridgeportart.com; 1200 W 35th St; admission free; 🚌8) – in revamped warehouses – hold the mother lode of galleries and workshops. The best time to visit is during the Third Friday Open Studios event (from 7pm to 10pm).

Best
Parks & Gardens

Chicago takes green space seriously. Since the 1830s its motto has been *Urbs in horto*, Latin for 'City in a Garden.' Almost the entire lakefront is public parkland, thanks to city planner Daniel Burnham. When he pieced the city together again after the Great Fire, he made sure enormous parks were part of the package.

Best for Strolling & Lolling

Millennium Park Meander around interactive public artworks, and bring a picnic for the evening concert. (p24)

Northerly Island The grassy park offers a tranquil escape from the nearby Museum Campus. (p118)

Best for Active Types

606 This old train track turned elevated path rolls through Wicker Park, Logan Square and onward. (p92)

Lincoln Park Join runners, rowers, walkers and cyclists in Chicago's largest green space. (p68)

Maggie Daley Park Blow off steam at the rock-climbing wall, ice-skating ribbon and whimsical playgrounds. (p34; pictured above right)

Best for People-Watching

Buckingham Fountain Everyone gathers around Grant Park's centerpiece for its trippy light shows and 15-story-high spout. (p34)

Mary Bartelme Park See how the West Loop's hipsters and families get their exercise. (p103)

☑ **Top Tip**

▶ The Chicago Park District (www.chicagoparkdistrict.com) lists all kinds of free events – movies, live music, theater – that take place in green spaces citywide.

Best Gardens

Lincoln Park Conservatory The small but potent dose of tropical blooms is especially welcome during winter. (p73)

Lurie Garden (p26) Find Millennium Park's secret garden and you're treated to a prairie's worth of wildflowers. (p26)

Best
Live Music

The birthplace of electric blues and house music, Chicago also fosters a rip-roaring independent rock scene, boundary-leaping jazz cats and all kinds of world beats. Venues are thick on the ground, with tunes spilling out of muggy clubs, sunny outdoor amphitheaters, DIY dive bars and everyplace in between.

Neighborhoods Hubs

Wicker Park and Logan Square hold the mother lode of cool little clubs where edgy indie bands plug in. Blues and jazz clubs are scattered around town, though a couple of big-name spots pop up in the South Loop. Lincoln Park offers convenient access to blues bars (especially on Halsted St) and intimate alternative venues.

DANIEL LADENHAUFF/500PX ©

☑ Top Tip

▶ See the alt-weekly *Chicago Reader* (www.chicagoreader.com) for comprehensive listings.

Best Blues

Buddy Guy's Legends Sick licks fill the air day and night. (p122)

BLUES Small, crackling club with seasoned local players. (p77)

Blue Chicago Handy Near North spot with good local acts. (p52)

Kingston Mines Hot and sweaty late-night venue with two stages jamming daily. (p77; pictured above right)

Best Jazz

Green Mill Big names in jazz bebop at this timeless tavern. (p87)

Whistler Artsy little club where indie bands and jazz trios brood. (p99)

Jazz Showcase Elegant room where national acts blow their horns. (p123)

Best Rock

Hideout Feels like your grandma's basement but with alt-country bands and literary readings. (p95)

Metro Cool buzz bands smash through sets. (p85)

Empty Bottle Go-to club for edgy indie rock. (p95)

Lincoln Hall Indie bands love to play the intimate room with pristine acoustics. (p77)

Best
**Sports &
Activities**

Chicago is a rabid sports town, and fans of the pro teams are famously die-hard. It's not all about passively watching sports, though. Chicago offers plenty of places to get active via its city-spanning shoreline, 26 beaches and 580 parks. After a long, cold winter, everyone goes outside to play.

JOHN KERSHNER/SHUTTERSTOCK ©

Lakefront Trail & Beaches

The flat, 18-mile Lakefront Trail is a beautiful route along the water, though on nice days it's jam-packed with runners and cyclists. It also connects the city's beaches. In summer lifeguards patrol the strands of sand. Swimming is popular, though the water is pretty freaking cold.

Best Spectator Sports

Chicago Cubs It's hard to beat a day at Wrigley Field in the sun-splashed bleachers. (p85)

Chicago Blackhawks Watching the city's hockey team is a raucous, beer-fueled good time. (p110)

Best Beaches

North Avenue Beach Party time at the boat-house and on the volley-ball courts. (p72)

Oak Street Beach Sandbox in the shadow of skyscrapers. (p62)

57th Street Beach Uncrowded South Side expanse and surfers' hub. (p125)

Best Guided Jaunts

Bobby's Bike Hike Groovy tours for children, and pizza and beer lovers. (p151)

Bike Chicago Excellent tours from Lincoln Park to Chinatown and Pilsen. (p151)

☑ **Top Tips**

▶ White Sox (www. whitesox.com) baseball tickets are usually cheaper and easier to get than Cubs tickets. The Sox (pictured above) play at Guaranteed Rate Field, 4 miles south of downtown and accessible via the El (Red Line to Sox-35th).

▶ For all teams, buy tickets direct from their website or stadium box office, or via StubHub (www. stubhub.com).

Urban Kayaks Rentals and tours launch downtown from the Riverwalk. (p36)

Best
Drinking & Nightlife

Chicagoans love to hang out in drinking establishments. Blame it on the long winter, when folks need to huddle together somewhere warm. Blame it on summer, when sunny days make beer gardens and sidewalk patios so splendid. Whatever the reason, drinking in the city is a widely cherished civic pastime.

BILL HOGAN/CHICAGO TRIBUNE/MCT VIA GETTY IMAGES ©

Clubs

Clubs cluster in three main areas: River North and West Loop, where the venues tend to be huge and luxurious, with dress codes; Wicker Park and Ukie Village, where they're typically more casual; and Wrigleyville and Boystown, where they fall somewhere in between.

How to Find a Real Chicago Bar

Look for the following: an old-style beer sign swinging out front; a well-worn dartboard and/or pool table inside; patrons wearing ballcaps with the logos of the Cubs, White Sox, Bears or Blackhawks; and sports on TV.

Best Vibe

Old Town Ale House Trendy tipplers and grizzled regulars sip under bawdy paintings. (p75)

RM Champagne Salon Twinkling West Loop spot that feels like a Parisian cafe. (p109)

Best Beer

Revolution Brewing Industrial-chic brewpub pouring righteous ales. (p99)

Delilah's Spirited punk bar with all kinds of odd ales (and whiskeys too). (p76)

Best Cocktails

Violet Hour Beard Award–winning cocktails in a hidden bar. (p94)

Arbella Drinks from around the globe served

☑ Top Tip

▶ The *Chicago Reader* (www.chicago reader.com) has bar and club listings.

in warm, cozy environs. (p51)

Best Views

Signature Lounge Ascend to the Hancock Center's 96th floor and gawp. (p64)

Cindy's Loop rooftop with vistas of Millennium Park. (p39)

Best Clubs

Smart Bar Intimate club that's serious about its DJs. (p84)

Berlin Welcome-one, welcome-all space to dance your ass off. (p84)

Best
For Kids

Ferocious dinosaurs at the Field Museum, an ark's worth of beasts at Lincoln Park Zoo, lakefront boat rides and sandy beaches are among the top choices for toddlin' times. Add in magical playgrounds, family cycling tours and lots of pizza, and it's clear Chicago is a kid's kind of town.

EQRODY/SHUTTERSTOCK ©

Best Museums

Chicago Children's Museum The slew of building, climbing and inventing exhibits keep young ones busy. (p49)

Museum of Science & Industry Kids can conduct 'research' in the Idea Factory. (p125)

Field Museum of Natural History The PlayLab lets tykes excavate bones and make other discoveries. (p114)

Peggy Notebaert Nature Museum The butterfly haven and marsh full of frogs provide gentle thrills. (p73)

Best Entertainment

Navy Pier The whirling swing, sky-high Ferris wheel, musical carousel – it's all here, plus boats. (p44)

Maggie Daley Park Enchanted forests and pirate-themed playgrounds. (p34)

Lincoln Park Zoo Swinging chimps, roaring lions and a barnyard full of farm animals to feed. (p72)

12th Street Beach Pint-sized waves are perfect for pint-sized swimmers. (p119)

Chicago Children's Theatre Quality shows, often adapted from kids' books. (p64)

Best Kids' Cuisine

Shake Shack Burgers, fries and milkshakes keep it simple and delicious. (p38)

Lou Mitchell's Free candy and doughnut holes supplement the plate-defying pancakes. (p106)

☑ **Top Tips**

▶ For kid-friendly happenings around town, see Chicago Kids (www.chicago kids.com).

▶ Bobby's Bike Hike (p151) and Bike Chicago (p151) rent children's bikes and bikes with child seats. Both also offer child-friendly tours.

Best Shops

American Girl Place Have tea and get a new hairdo with your doll. (p65)

Lego Store So many cool things to build at the hands-on tables. (p65; pictured above)

Best
Gay & Lesbian

Chicago has a flourishing gay and lesbian scene. The biggest concentration of bars and clubs is in Wrigleyville on N Halsted St between Belmont Ave and Grace St, a party-hearty area known as Boystown (pictured right). Andersonville is the other main area for LGBT nightlife. It's a more relaxed, less party-oriented atmosphere.

DAVID TIDWELL 86/GETTY IMAGES ©

Festivals

The main event on the calendar is the **Pride Parade** (www.chicagopride.gopride.com), held the last Sunday in June. It winds through Boystown and attracts more than 800,000 risqué revelers. **Northalsted Market Days** (www.northalsted.com), another wild time in Boystown, is a steamy two-day street fair in mid-August. Crafty, incense-wafting vendors line Halsted St, but most folks come for the drag queens in feather boas, Twister games played in the street and disco divas (Gloria Gaynor!) on the main stage. The **International Mr Leather** (www.imrl. com) contest brings out lots of men in, well, leather in late May. Workshops and parties take place around town, with the main event happening at a downtown hotel or theater.

☑ **Top Tip**

▶ Windy City Times (www.windycity mediagroup.com) is the main source for LGBTQI events and entertainment.

Sidetrack Thumping dance music, show tune sing-alongs and prime people-watching. (p84)

Hamburger Mary's Cabaret, karaoke, burgers and a booze-soaked outdoor patio for good times. (p87)

Berlin Longstanding club where party people dance until the wee hours. (p84)

Closet A small, laid-back bar for ladies until the boys crash late at night. (p84)

Home Bistro Bring your own wine and settle in for nouveau comfort food in Boystown's center. (p83)

Best
Comedy &
Performing Arts

Improv comedy was born in Chicago, and the city still nurtures the best in the biz. Chicago's reputation for stage drama is well deserved, with Hollywood-star-laden Steppenwolf among the 200 local theaters. Many productions export to Broadway, while many play in fringy 'off-Loop' storefronts. The symphony and opera also draw worldwide accolades.

Improv

US improv started in a Hyde Park bar in 1955 with the Compass Players. Their original gag was to use audience suggestions in their quick-witted routine. They went on to found Second City, and their style of unstructured, spectator-fueled skits went viral.

Theater District

Chicago's Theater District is a group of century-old, neon-lit playhouses that cluster at State and Randolph Sts. They usually host big touring productions.

Best Comedy

Second City The improv bastion that's launched many a jokester's career. (p76)

iO Theater This good-time, four-theater improv house has sent many on to stardom. (p76)

Best Theater

Steppenwolf Theatre Drama club of Malkovich, Sinise and other Hollywood stars. (p76)

Goodman Theatre Excellent new and classic American plays. (p39)

Best Classical & Opera

Grant Park Orchestra Everyone's favorite group to picnic with at Pritzker Pavilion. (p39)

Chicago Symphony Orchestra World-renowned, with a smokin' brass section. (p39)

Lyric Opera High Cs in a chandeliered venue. (p41)

Best Dance

SummerDance Locals young and old come out for free world music concerts and dance lessons. (p118)

Hubbard Street Dance Chicago Foremost modern troupe in town. (p41)

ANDREY BAYDA/SHUTTERSTOCK ©

☑ **Top Tip**

▶ Hot Tix (www.hottix.org) sells same-week drama, comedy and performing-arts tickets for half price (plus a $5 to $10 service charge). The selection is best early in the week.

Best
Shopping

ROSA IRENE BETANCOURT 7/ALAMY STOCK PHOTO ©

From the glossy stores of the Magnificent Mile to the countercultural shops of Lake View to the indie designers of Wicker Park, Chicago is a shopper's destination. It has been that way from the get-go. After all, this is the city that birthed the department store and traditions such as the money-back guarantee, bridal registry and bargain basement.

Specialties

Music is big. Independent record stores flood Chicago's neighborhoods, supported by the thriving live-music scene in town. Vinyl geeks will find heaps of stacks to flip through. Vintage and thrift fashions are another claim to fame. Art- and architecture-related items are another Chicago specialty.

Best Music

Reckless Records Great place to get the scoop on local indie rock bands. (p96)

Dusty Groove Killer stacks of vinyl hold rare soul and funk beats. (p97)

Dave's Records *Rolling Stone* magazine dubbed it one of the nation's best shops. (p77)

Best Books

Quimby's Ground zero for comics, zines and underground culture. (p96)

Seminary Co-op Bookstore Brainy shop beloved by Nobel Prize winners. (p125; pictured above right)

Best Souvenirs

Chicago Architecture Foundation Shop Pick up a mini Willis Tower model or skyline poster. (p41)

Strange Cargo Huge array of iconic T-shirts, from the El to a Chicago-style hot-dog diagram. (p85)

Best Fashion & Vintage

Knee Deep Vintage Groovy garb and home-wares from the 1920s to the 1970s. (p111)

Una Mae's Emerge looking all Jackie O in your new old hat. (p96)

Best Local

Woolly Mammoth Antiques & Oddities That jar of old dentures? Here, beside the stuffed wallaby. (p87)

Wolfbait & B-girls Local designers sew wares on site. (p99)

Best
Tours

Chicago offers loads of tours. Boat excursions are the most popular way to go. The skyline takes on a surreal majesty as you float through its shadows on the Chicago River. Jaunts by foot, bus or bicycle are great for exploring off-the-beaten-path neighborhoods or delving into a particular topic of interest, such as art-deco buildings, gangster sites or breweries.

JESSICA KIRSH/SHUTTERSTOCK ©

Chicago Architecture Foundation (CAF; ☎312-922-3432; www.architecture.org; 224 S Michigan Ave; tours $15-50; Ⓜ Brown, Orange, Green, Purple, Pink Line to Adams) The gold-standard boat tours ($46) sail from the river dock on the southeast side of the Michigan Ave Bridge. The popular Historic Skyscrapers walking tours ($20) leave from the main downtown address. Buy tickets online or at CAF.

Chicago by Foot (☎312-612-0826; www.freetoursbyfoot.com/chicago-tours) Guides for this pay-what-you-want walking tour offer engaging stories and historical details on different jaunts covering the Loop, Gold Coast, Lincoln Park's gangster sites and much more.

Most takers pay around $10 per person. Reserve in advance to guarantee a spot.

Chicago Detours (☎312-350-1131; www.chicagodetours.com; tours from $22) It offers engrossing, detail-rich tours (mostly walking, but also some by bus) that take in Chicago's architecture, history and culture. The 2½-hour Historic Pub Crawl Tour is a popular one.

InstaGreeter (www.chicagogreeter.com/instagreeter; 77 E Randolph St; admission free; ⊙10am-3pm Fri & Sat, 11am-2pm Sun; Ⓜ Brown, Orange, Green, Purple, Pink Line to Washington/Wabash) It provides one-hour Loop tours from the Chicago Cultural Center. No bookings are taken; just show up in

the Randolph St lobby. In summer, free tours of Millennium Park also depart from here daily at 11:30am and 1pm.

Chicago Food Planet Tours (☎312-818-2170; www.chicagofoodplanet.com; 2-3hr tours $42-65) Go on a guided walkabout in Wicker Park, the Gold Coast or Chinatown, where you'll graze through five or more neighborhood eateries. Departure points and times vary.

☑ **Top Tips**

▶ Many companies offer discounts if you book online.

▶ Most outdoor-oriented tours operate from April to November only.

Survival Guide

Survival Guide

Before You Go

When to Go

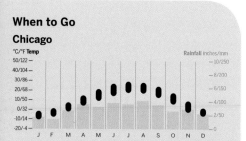

Chicago

°C/°F Temp
50/122 —
40/104 —
30/86 —
20/68 —
10/50 —
0/32 —
-10/14 —
-20/-4 —

Rainfall inches/mm
— 10/250
— 8/200
— 6/150
— 4/100
— 2/50
— 0

J F M A M J J A S O N D

➡ **Winter** (Dec–Feb) December twinkles with holiday festivals. Otherwise it's gray, snowy, cold with low-season bargains.

➡ **Spring** (Mar–May) Still chilly, though gorgeous days sprinkle in – prime for catching a baseball game.

➡ **Summer** (Jun–Aug) Peak tourism season thanks to warm weather and festivals. Can be hot and humid, but usually comfy.

➡ **Autumn** (Sep–Nov) Shoulder season. Lodging prices decrease. Football, hockey and basketball ramp up.

Book Your Stay

➡ The Loop and Near North are the most lodging-filled neighborhoods.

➡ Chicago's 17.4% hotel tax is not included in most quoted rates.

➡ For parking costs, figure on $55 to $65 per night downtown ($25 per night in outlying neighborhoods).

Useful Websites

➡ **Lonely Planet** (www. lonelyplanet.com/hotels) Recommendations and bookings.

➡ **Chicago Bed & Breakfast Association** (www. chicago-bed-breakfast. com) Represents around 10 properties.

➡ **Hotel Tonight** (www. hoteltonight.com) National discounter with last-minute deals; book via the free app.

➡ **Choose Chicago** (www. choosechicago.com)

Options from the city's official website.

Best Budget

⇒ Fieldhouse Jones
(www.fieldhousejones. com) Sporty, companionable digs for an unrivaled Gold Coast price.

⇒ Hollander
(www.the hollander.com) Posh hostel in the thick of Wicker Park's social scene.

⇒ Holiday Jones
(www. holidayjones.com) Good-value, off-the-beaten-path hostel with a sense of humor.

⇒ Freehand Chicago
(www.thefreehand.com/ chicago) Super-hip hostel-hotel hybrid with spiffy, high-tech dorms.

⇒ HI-Chicago
(www. hichicago.org) You can't beat the Loop location and free city tours.

Best Midrange

⇒ Acme Hotel
(www. acmehotelcompany.com) Tech-ed up, rock-and-roll hot spot for urban bohemians.

⇒ Hampton Inn Chicago Downtown/N Loop
(www.hamptonchicago. com) The chain's much-loved amenities in retro, charismatic environs.

⇒ Longman & Eagle
(www.longmananeagle. com) A true tavern with unassuming, epicurean food below and low-key, cool-cat rooms above.

⇒ Hotel Lincoln
(www. jdvhotels.com) Fun, from 'wall of bad art' kitsch to pedicab service.

⇒ Buckingham Athletic Club Hotel
(www.the buckinghamclub.com) Expansive rooms and a gym with lap pool, hiding downtown.

⇒ Willows Hotel
(www. willowshotelchicago. com) Peachy rooms fill this dapper little property.

Best Top End

⇒ Virgin Hotel
(www. virginhotels.com) Large rooms, clever and playful design, and a bed you can work from.

⇒ Guesthouse Hotel
(www.theguesthouse hotel.com) Enormous modern suites near Andersonville's hip shops and taverns.

⇒ Radisson Blu Aqua Hotel
(www.radissonblu. com/aquahotel-chicago) Mod, blond-wood rooms with balconies and views.

⇒ Drake Hotel
(www.the drakehotel.com) Historic gilded property at the head of the Magnificent Mile.

Arriving in Chicago

O'Hare International Airport

⇒ Train
The airport has its own El train station on the Blue Line operated by the Chicago Transit Authority (www. transitchicago.com). Trains run 24/7 and cost $5. They depart every 10 minutes or so and reach downtown in 40 minutes.

⇒ Shuttle van
The GO Airport Express (www. airportexpress.com) shared-van service goes downtown for $35 per person. Vans run between 4am and 11:30pm, departing every 15 minutes. It takes an hour or more, depending on traffic and where your hotel is in the drop-off order.

⇒ Taxi
Rides to the center take 30 minutes and cost

around $50. Taxi queues can be lengthy, and the ride can take longer than the train, depending on traffic.

Chicago Midway Airport

➡ **Train** The airport has its own El train station on the Orange Line operated by the Chicago Transit Authority (www.transit chicago.com). Trains run between 4am and 1am and cost $3. They depart every 10 minutes or so and reach downtown in 30 minutes.

➡ **Shuttle van** The GO Airport Express (www. airportexpress.com) door-to-door shuttle goes downtown for $30. Vans run between 4am and 10:30pm. The journey takes approximately 50 minutes.

➡ **Taxi** Rides to the center take 20 minutes or longer (depending on traffic) and cost $35 to $40.

Union Station

➡ **Train** For public transportation onward, the Blue Line Clinton stop is a few blocks south (though it's not a good option at night). The Brown, Orange, Purple and Pink Line station at Quincy is about a half-mile east.

➡ **Taxi** Taxis queue along Canal St outside the station entrance.

Getting Around

Elevated/Subway Train

➡ The El (it stands for 'elevated,' though many trains also run underground; www. transitchicago.com) is fast, frequent and will get you to most sights and neighborhoods.

➡ Two of the eight color-coded lines – the Red Line, and the Blue Line to O'Hare airport – operate 24 hours a day. The other lines run from 4am to 1am daily, departing every 10 minutes or so.

➡ The standard fare is $3 (except from O'Hare airport, where it costs $5) and includes two transfers.

➡ Enter the turnstile using a Ventra Ticket, which is sold from vending machines at train stations.

➡ You can also buy a Ventra Card, aka a rechargeable fare card, at stations It has a one-time $5 fee that gets refunded once you register the card. It knocks around 75¢ off the cost of each ride.

Bus

➡ City buses operate from early morning until late evening.

➡ The fare is $2 ($2.25 if you want a transfer).

➡ You can use a Ventra Card or pay the driver with exact change.

➡ Buses are particularly useful for reaching the Museum Campus, Hyde Park and Lincoln Park's zoo.

Taxi

➡ Taxis are plentiful in the Loop, north to Andersonville and northwest to Wicker Park/Bucktown.

➡ Fares are meter-based and start at $3.25 when you get into the cab, then it's $2.25 per mile. The first extra passenger costs $1; extra passengers after that are 50¢ apiece.

➡ Try **Checker Taxi** (📞312-243-2537; www. checkertaxichicago.com) if you need a pick-up.

The ride-sharing companies Uber, Lyft and Via are also popular in Chicago.

Bicycle

→ Divvy (www.divvybikes. com) has 5800 sky-blue bikes at 580 stations around Chicago and neighboring suburbs.

→ Kiosks issue 24-hour passes ($10) on the spot. Insert a credit card, get your ride code, then unlock a bike.

→ The first 30 minutes are free; after that, rates rise fast if you don't dock the bike.

→ Bike rentals for longer rides (with accoutrements such as helmets and locks) start at around $18 for two hours. Try **Bike Chicago** (Map p32; ☏312-729-1000; www.bike chicago.com; 239 E Randolph St; bikes per hour/day from $9/30; ◷6:30am-10pm Mon-Fri, from 8am Sat & Sun Jun-Aug, reduced hours rest of year; Ⓜ Brown, Orange, Green, Purple, Pink Line to Washington/Wabash) or **Bobby's Bike Hike** (Map p46; ☏312-245-9300; www. bobbysbikehike.com; 540 N Lake Shore Dr; per hour/day from $10/34; ◷8:30am-8pm Mon-Fri, 8am-8pm Sat & Sun

Money-Saving Tips

→ If you're going to use the El more than a few times, it's worth it to buy a rechargeable Ventra Card, available at any station. You can add value as needed. Without a Ventra Card, each ride you take is subject to a surcharge for using a disposable ticket.

→ Unlimited ride passes (one-/three-day pass $10/20) are also available; get them at train stations.

→ Hottix (www.hottix.org) sells drama, comedy and performing-arts tickets for half-price.

Jun-Aug, 9am-7pm Mar-May & Sep-Nov; Ⓜ Red Line to Grand).

Car & Motorcycle

→ Traffic is often jammed, and street parking is scarce.

→ Downtown garages cost about $40 per day.

→ On-street, metered parking costs from $2 per hour (in outlying areas) to $6.50 per hour (in the Loop).

→ Note that 'meter' is a bit of a misnomer – you actually feed coins or a credit card into a pay box that serves the entire block.

→ Some meter-free neighborhoods require resident parking passes,

and some don't. Read signs carefully.

Essential Information

Business Hours

Typical normal opening times are as follows:

Banks & businesses 9am–5pm Monday–Friday

Bars 5pm–2am (to 3am on Saturday); some licensed until 4am (to 5am on Saturday)

Nightclubs 10pm–4am; often closed Monday through Wednesday

Restaurants Breakfast 7am or 8am–11am, lunch 11am or 11:30am–2:30pm, dinner 5pm or 6pm–10pm Sunday–Thursday, to 11pm or midnight Friday and Saturday

Shops 11am–7pm Monday–Saturday, noon–6pm Sunday

Discount Cards

➡ The **Go Chicago Card** (www.smartdestinations.com/chicago) allows you to visit an unlimited number of attractions for a flat fee. It's good for one, two, three or five consecutive days.

➡ The company also offers a three-, four- or five-choice 'Explorer Pass' where you pick among 25 options for sights. It's valid for 30 days.

➡ **CityPass** (www.citypass.com/chicago) gives access to five of the city's top draws, including the Art Institute, Shedd Aquarium and Willis Tower, over nine days. It's less flexible than Go Chicago's pass, but cheaper for those wanting a more leisurely sightseeing pace.

➡ All of the above let you skip the regular queues at sights.

Electricity

Type A
120V/60Hz

Type B
120V/60Hz

Money

ATMs

➡ ATMs are widely available 24/7

➡ Most ATMs link into worldwide networks (Plus, Cirrus, Exchange etc).

➡ ATMs typically charge a service fee of $3 or more per transaction.

Credit Cards

Visa, MasterCard and American Express are widely accepted at hotels, restaurants, bars and shops.

Tipping

Tipping is not optional; only withhold tips in cases of outrageously bad service.

Airport & hotel porters $2 per bag, minimum per cart $5

Bartenders 15% per round, minimum per drink $1

Housekeeping staff $2 to $5 per night

Restaurant servers 15% to 20%, unless gratuity is already included on bill

Taxi drivers 10% to 15%, rounded up to the next dollar

Parking valets $2 to $5 when you collect the keys.

Public Holidays

Banks, schools, offices and most shops close on these days:

New Year's Day January 1

Martin Luther King Jr Day Third Monday in January

President's Day Third Monday in February

Pulaski Day First Monday in March (observed mostly by city offices)

Memorial Day Last Monday in May

Independence Day July 4

Labor Day First Monday in September

Columbus Day Second Monday in October

Veteran's Day November 11

Thanksgiving Day Fourth Thursday in November

Christmas Day December 25

Telephone

US country code ☎ 1

Chicago area codes ☎ 312, 773, 872

Making international calls Dial ☎ 011 + country code + area code + local number

Calling other US area codes or Canada Dial ☎ 1 + area code + seven-digit local number

Calling within Chicago Dial ☎ 1 + area code + seven-digit local number. It works the same whether you're calling a landline or cell phone

Travelers with Disabilities

➡ Most museums and major sights are wheelchair accessible, as are most large hotels and restaurants.

➡ All city buses are wheelchair accessible, but about one-third of El stations are not.

➡ Easy Access Chicago (www.easyaccesschicago. org) is a free resource that lists museums, tours, restaurants and lodgings, and provides mobility, vision and hearing accessibility information for each place.

Visas

➡ The Visa Waiver Program (VWP) allows nationals from some 36 countries (including most EU countries, Japan, Australia and New Zealand) to enter the US without a visa for up to 90 days.

➡ VWP visitors need an e-passport (with electronic chip) and approval under the Electronic System For Travel Authorization at least three days before arrival. There's a $14 fee for processing and authorization (payable online). Once approved, registration is valid for two years.

➡ Anyone staying longer than 90 days, or from a non-VWP country should apply at the US consulate in their home country.

Dos & Don'ts

Smoking Don't smoke in restaurants or bars: Chicago is smoke-free by law in those venues.

Dining Most people eat dinner between 6pm and 8pm (a bit later if dining out).

On escalators Stand to the right on the escalators; walk on the left.

Ketchup on a hot dog Don't do it! It's a local quirk that the red sauce doesn't go on wieners.

Behind the Scenes

Send Us Your Feedback

We love to hear from travelers – your comments help make our books better. We read every word, and we guarantee that your feedback goes straight to the authors. Visit **lonelyplanet.com/contact** to submit your updates and suggestions.

Note: We may edit, reproduce and incorporate your comments in Lonely Planet products such as guidebooks, websites and digital products, so let us know if you don't want your comments reproduced or your name acknowledged. For a copy of our privacy policy visit lonelyplanet.com/privacy.

Karla's Thanks

Many thanks to all of my Chicago friends who took the time to share their favorite local spots and join me for a beverage. Special thanks to Eric Markowitz, the world's best partner-for-life, who indulges my beer- and doughnut-filled ramblings with an endless supply of good humor.

Acknowledgements

Cover photograph: Skyline from North Avenue Beach, Birgit Tyrell/Alamy © Photograph on pp4–5: Downtown Chicago, ghornephoto/Getty Images ©

This Book

This third edition of Lonely Planet's *Pocket Chicago* guidebook was researched and written by Karla Zimmerman.

This guidebook was produced by the following:

Destination Editors Lauren Keith, Trisha Ping

Product Editors Sandie Kestell, Genna Patterson

Senior Cartographer Alison Lyall

Book Designer Gwen Cotter

Assisting Editors Imogen Bannister, Pete Cruttenden, Gabrielle Innes

Assisting Cartographer Julie Dodkins

Cover Researcher Marika Mercer

Thanks to Grace Dobell, Jessica Ryan, Angela Tinson, Tony Wheeler

Index

See also separate subindexes for:

🌀 Eating p157

🍷 Drinking p157

✪ Entertainment p158

🔒 Shopping p158

Sights 000
Map Pages **000**

Our Writer

Karla Zimmerman

Karla lives in Chicago, where she eats doughnuts, yells at the Cubs, and writes stuff for books, magazines, and websites when she's not doing the first two things. She has contributed to 40-plus guidebooks and travel anthologies covering destinations in Europe, Asia, Africa, North America, and the Caribbean – all of which are a long way from the early days, when she wrote about gravel for a construction magazine and got to trek to places like Fredon' ... To learn more, follow her on Instagram and Tw

WITHDRAWN

Published by Lonely Planet Global Limited
CRN 554153
3rd edition – Dec 2017
ISBN 978 1 78657 353 7
© Lonely Planet 2017 Photographs © as indicated 2017
10 9 8 7 6 5 4 3 2 1
Printed in Singapore

Although the ... ely Planet have taken all reasonable care in preparing this book, we make no warranty about the accuracy or completeness of its content and, to the maximum extent permitted, disclaim all liability arising from its use.

All rights reserved. No part of this publication may be copied, stored in a retrieval system, or transmitted in any form by any means, electronic, mechanical, recording or otherwise, except brief extracts for the purpose of review, and no part of this publication may be sold or hired, without the written permission of the publisher. Lonely Planet and the Lonely Planet logo are trademarks of Lonely Planet and are registered in the US Patent and Trademark Office and in other countries. Lonely Planet does not allow its name or logo to be appropriated by commercial establishments, such as retailers, restaurants or hotels. Please let us know of any misuses: lonelyplanet.com/ip.